**Federal Business
Development Bank**

Banque fédérale
de développement

MINDING
YOUR OWN BUSINESS

Volume I

Published by
FEDERAL BUSINESS DEVELOPMENT BANK

© Federal Business Development Bank, 1974, 1982

First edition December 1974
Second edition August 1977
Third edition February 1979
Revised edition March 1982

Federal Business Development Bank
901 Victoria Square
Montreal, Quebec,
Canada

ISSN 0708-6121
ISBN-0-662-11984-3

Publié aussi en français

CONTENTS

FOREWORD

Small business is the driving force in the Canadian economy in terms of both output and employment. Collectively, small business is estimated to account for 25 percent of the gross national product and 42 percent of Canada's work force. There are more than 900,000 small businesses in Canada. They comprise sole proprietorships, family businesses and partnerships, small corporations, the self-employed, and professionals. It can be safely said that the majority of businesses in this country are small and independently owned.

It can also be safely said that a special characteristic of small business is its functional management. In many instances, one owner/manager manages every aspect of the business. This person, rarely a master of all management skills, has to be a general manager, sales manager, production manager, purchasing manager, personnel manager, controller, and research manager for the business, especially during its early years. It helps if the owner/manager understands marketing, quality controls, finance, banking, commercial law, and human relations.

This volume cannot be an exhaustive text on all that the small business owner must know. It does, however, introduce various concepts of financial and administrative management that are particularly important to small business.

The material in this book originally appeared as Pamphlet Nos. 2 to 14 in the series "Minding Your Own Business". This present volume has subsequently been revised, re-written, and updated with additional information so as to increase its usefulness for the prospective entrepreneur and the established owner/manager.

Since 1974, almost five million copies of "Minding Your Own Business" have been distributed to owners and managers of small businesses in Canada. It is hoped that this new edition of the pocketbook will prove to be just as popular and as helpful.

1. FORECASTING FOR AN EXISTING BUSINESS

"A forecast is one of the most useful tools the entrepreneur has in planning the future course of his or her business."

— *CASE Counsellor*

INTRODUCTION

Tomorrow's uncertainties are something with which we must all live. Often, a small business is more vulnerable to the uncertainties of the future than is the larger business. Although exact knowledge of the future is unobtainable, an idea of what to expect can be very helpful for the small business operator.

At best, you can estimate or forecast what you **think** may happen. Although this may seem like a guessing game, it can well result in changing the course of your business's future. In short, predicting what may happen helps reduce your uncertainties.

This chapter will show you why preparing a realistic forecast is important to your business. We will begin by defining forecasting and then explain its value. As well, this chapter will give you pointers on how to prepare a forecast.

WHAT IS FORECASTING?

Forecasting will help you estimate your business's activities both financially and strategically.

1. Financially, forecasting means estimating the revenues, expenses and profits that your business will incur in a certain period of time in the future.

2. Strategically, a forecast can indicate the areas for growth and expansion whether in facilities or in products. A forecast can also point out activities that may need strengthening.

Generally, a forecast is prepared for a one-year period — the year following the year-end of the business's financial statements. This does not mean that forecasts should be prepared for only one-year periods. Many businesses find it very useful to prepare a one-year forecast and then divide it into shorter periods — say three to six months. In planning for the longer term, forecasts are often prepared for periods of two to five years in the future.

Having past financial records is the advantage that the existing business has over the new business. There is a distinct relationship between your business's past and its future. The information from past records can help you plan realistically for the future. Knowing where your business has been will help you determine where your business is going. However, your forecast must not be built solely upon the past; you must determine, as well, what changes you wish to occur in your business so as to provide input for the future and to help ensure growth.

Because forecasting involves a certain amount of guessing it is crucial that the forecaster has good, sound judgement. What you are doing, as the forecaster, is carefully combining objective data (your past records and known expenses) with subjective inferences about what you think the future may bring. To blend the two takes experience, not just academic knowledge.

WHAT IS THE VALUE OF FORECASTING?

Preparing an operating forecast does not necessarily have to be time consuming. At any rate, the benefits you derive are well worth your time and effort. Let us take a look at some of the advantages a forecasting statement will provide:

(a) A realistic forecast will point to what new facilities or expansions are needed. Because it gives you an opportunity to study the business's past results in detail, it may disclose opportunities to expand the business which might not be apparent during the hectic day-to-day operations of the business. Let us suppose that a motel/restaurant operator is studying her business's previous operating history. She might find that revenues from her small restaurant have been increasing quite substantially, even though there has not been any noticeable increase in the occupancy rate of her motel. The increase in restaurant revenues, if extended into the next year and subsequent years, might well cause this operator to examine the restaurant situation very closely and to give consideration to its expansion.

(b) Forecasting will not only help determine what new expansions are available, it will also allow you to plan and schedule them. In other words, you may then make arrangements, or determine the feasibility, for obtaining the necessary capital to realize these plans. You may also wish to consider your various alternatives. For example: buying or leasing certain assets; putting up a new building or renovating the old one; changing the variety of products sold or produced.

(c) Again because it requires a study of past experience, preparing a forecast can help in drawing the business operator's attention to certain expenses which should be watched closely.

(d) Comparing a forecast with the results actually experienced will not only help in pointing out areas of opportunity but also those of concern. In looking ahead, preparing a forecast may help detect a problem before it is too late. For example, you may find that in spite of increasing revenues, profits have actually been slightly declining. Recognizing this slow decline today could prevent you from suddenly being unable to meet expenses or to make necessary purchases tomorrow. Such a situation would result in an analysis of your expenses to determine which of them were increasing and where reductions could be made.

The main point to remember is that a forecast is a tool that will help reduce your business's uncertainties by realistically determining, as accurately as possible, what factors may play a role in your business's future.

HOW TO PREPARE THE FORECAST

Before starting a forecast, it is important that you prepare it on the basis of what your business has done and what your business can **reasonably** be expected to do. There can be a considerable difference between what your business is expected to achieve in the future and what you would like it to achieve. Naturally, we would all like to see our profits triple in one year. Realistically though, this is not very probable. It is essential that you keep this in mind while preparing your forecast.

Perhaps the first step in putting together a forecast is that you establish your objectives. In other words, that you know why you are forecasting. This is the only way your statement will have any value. Defining your objective will also indicate for what length of time you are going to forecast. If you are forecasting for the purchase of materials, you may plan a forecast for a year as opposed to a long-term forecast for capital expenditures which could cover a period of two to five years.

Your second step is to gather all pertinent information and data. Work with your business's most recent statements. Establish all the changes that you can realistically expect to occur in your business within the time frame of your forecast.

Now that both your objective and expectations have been determined, you can begin the third step: actually preparing your forecast. Your forecast will be an estimate of the following:

- sales
- cost of goods sold
- gross margin
- operating expenses
- profits

Let us examine each one in turn.

Sales In forecasting your sales, the logical starting point is your last year's sales figures. Quite often, identifying past trends will point to future ones. For example, if over the last two years your sales have increased by 15 percent, it is usually safe to assume that, given similar conditions, your sales figure for the year that you are forecasting will again increase by the same percentage. Of course, if you have plans that could affect your sales such as the introduction of a new product, changes in location, or a major advertising and promotion campaign, this percentage will have to be adjusted.

External factors must also be considered when forecasting your sales. In other words, you must analyze your market with questions such as: Is my share of the market growing or declining? Are there more or fewer competitors? What are they charging for the same or similar product? And you must recognize the effect of inflation, possible price increases, and the availability of inventory.

If you divide your forecast into months, your past monthly sales records will show you which months are more active than others. This trend may continue or be adjusted by known external factors or by the previously mentioned internal events such as an advertising campaign or the release of a new product.

It must be stressed that your sales forecast be as realistic as is possible. Too often, small business entrepreneurs, while showing realism in estimating cost of goods sold and expenses, will reflect too high an optimism in forecasting their sales.

Cost of Goods Sold   There has to be a direct relationship between your forecast of sales and the cost of goods that you plan to sell. What if you are able to determine from previous years' figures that, say, 80 percent of your sales figure represents cost of goods sold? For many small businesses, you could then simply calculate future cost of goods sold by taking 80 percent of future sales.

For larger retailers and for most manufacturers, cost of goods sold must consider planned inventory levels. The retailer will want to be sure that there is a proper stock turnover rate that is related to sales. The manufacturer will be concerned that proper inventory levels in finished goods, goods in process, and raw materials have an accurate relationship to the sales forecast.

Gross Margin   In simple terms, gross margin is determined by subtracting cost of goods sold from sales.

Operating Expenses   Operating expenses are usually termed fixed and variable. Fixed expenses, such as rent and depreciation, are those required for the normal operation of your business. Variable expenses, such as advertising and wages, are those that will vary because of their close relationship to your sales. An increase in sales may be reflected in increased advertising expenses and additional staff. For the manufacturer, there will be a relationship between overhead, labour, and sales.

Your previous years' figures will help you forecast your operating expenses. For example, a steady 10 to 15 percent increase over the last couple of years can be a realistic factor to use in forecasting the next year's operating expenses. As we saw when forecasting sales, both external factors and planned internal events will affect your forecast of operating expenses.

Profit Subtracting your operating expenses from gross margin will give you the forecasted profit for your business.

To further explain a forecast, we show a profit and loss statement for a small business's fourth year in operation and the forecast prepared by the owner for the future — the fifth year. Here are some facts on our hypothetical small business:

The business operates from leased premises. The rental is $800 a month with the landlord paying utilities and realty taxes but not business taxes. The owner is thinking of buying a building instead of the present lease arrangements.

Additional space in the new premises will permit the carrying of additional lines. The new location will also mean more customers. Business revenues are expected to increase from $300,000 to $350,000. Cost of goods sold over the last four years has been 80 percent. The building will cost $35,000 and the land $15,000. A loan of $30,000 will be arranged at the current interest rate.

Profit and Loss Statement
for Fourth Year

Sales		$300,000
Cost of Goods Sold		240,000
Gross Margin		60,000
Operating Expenses:		
Wages — part-time clerk	$10,000	
Salary — owner	20,000	
Overhead	nil	
Depreciation — fixtures	1,000	
Delivery expenses	3,000	
Telephone	400	
Interest	300	
Insurance	500	
Advertising	2,000	
Delivery vehicle repairs	675	
Bad debt expenses	500	
Rent — $800 per month	9,600	
Business taxes	400	
Realty taxes	nil	
Total Operating Expenses		48,375
Profit before Taxes		11,625

Forecast for Fifth Year

Sales		$350,000
Cost of Goods Sold		280,000
Gross Margin		70,000

Operating Expenses:

Wages — part-time clerk	$12,000	
Salary — owner	22,000	
Overhead	2,000 [1]	
Depreciation — fixtures	1,000	
Depreciation — building	1,250 [2]	
Delivery expenses	3,500 [3]	
Telephone	400	
Interest	2,000	
Advertising	2,000	
Delivery vehicle repairs	750	
Bad debt expenses	750 [4]	
Rent	nil [5]	
Business taxes	400	
Realty taxes	800 [6]	
Total Operating Expenses		48,850
Profit before Taxes		21,150

NOTES:

1. Owner no longer has a landlord to pay heating and upkeep on premises — business must now pay.
2. Building depreciated ($35,000 over 20 years) over the length of the loan.
3. Delivery expense increases because of increased business.
4. Bad debt expense increases because more credit given.
5. Rent no longer paid (loan payments not an expense but interest is).
6. Realty taxes now payable because business owns property.

CONCLUSION

Forecasts are necessary for the successful small business. For almost every business, a forecast is required. If a formal forecast is not prepared, decision-making on all future activities — an increase in ordering of inventory, the purchase of equipment and supplies, the hiring of people, the plans for expansion — will be undertaken piecemeal. This will result in no overall vision and will have a high potential for error. By preparing a forecast, actual results can be compared to the forecast on a monthly or quarterly basis and problem areas can be quickly identified.

2. FORECASTING FOR A NEW BUSINESS

"Forecasting is more difficult without past records, but a new business still needs to forecast."

— *CASE Counsellor*

INTRODUCTION

In our previous chapter, we examined the concept of forecasting and related it to the existing business. We saw the benefits of past financial records and saw how, to a considerable degree, they were the basis for preparing a forecast. But how does the new business forecast when it has just begun operations and has no past financial records? What about the new business that has not begun operating — how does it prepare a forecast?

The purpose of this chapter is to show the need for a new business to forecast, to examine the difficulties facing the new entrepreneur when called upon to estimate the future, and to provide some pointers in putting together the first forecast.

DOES A NEW BUSINESS NEED A FORECAST?

A forecast is one of the most useful tools the entrepreneur has in planning the future course of his or her business. For the new business that is just about to start, or for the entrepreneur who is wondering whether or not it makes financial sense to start a new business, preparing a forecast can be considered mandatory.

Basically, there are two reasons for preparing that first forecast:

1. To ascertain for yourself if the business venture will be viable; to visualize your business on paper so as to determine if there are any weaknesses, and to find out if there will be a profit and what the probable amount will be.

2. To demonstrate to a lender and/or outside investor that your new business venture is sound and that any monies put into the business will not be lost. The lender will want to be assured repayment with interest and the investor will want to be sure that there is a good return on investment.

The need for a forecast can be clearly shown in the following situation:

David Miller has been a first class mechanic for over fifteen years. He has spent ten of these years working at a large dealership on Main Street. David has always had an affinity with cars, especially English and foreign sports cars. In fact, the sole reason why so many customers who own foreign sports cars are coming to the dealership is because of David's expertise. Another factor is that there is no top quality foreign car service available in the town.

This has made David Miller realize his importance and has given him the idea of opening his own garage specializing in sports cars. He has some savings, but feels it will not be enough, so he approached a very good friend, Jim Banes.

"I tell you," said David, "we can't lose. Look at the number of foreign sports cars in the area. And don't forget what happens during the summer when all the tourists pass through. There's nobody specializing in repairing these cars."

"I know what you are saying is true, but how do we really know we can make a go of it?" asked Jim cautiously.

"Look, we'll buy that closed gas station just outside of town. It's going cheap. We'll get rid of the pumps, put in two pits in the bays, buy some equipment, get some supplies and some stock..."

"Wait a moment," interrupted Jim. "I'm not putting any money in until I know how much money I'll make; especially in the first year and then for the next five. How do I know I won't make more by keeping my money in five year Canada Savings Bonds?"

David was exasperated. He knew he'd make a go of it, but how was he going to show Jim how much he'd make each year? David decided to go to the bank manager whom he'd known for over 15 years.

"Sorry David," said the manager. "I can't tell you now if we'd loan you the money. I must have some statements from you first — an estimate of what your business will do."

"I don't understand," replied David. "I'm not in business yet. How can I tell you how much I'll make each year in the future?"

The bank manager explained to David how to prepare a forecast. This explanation can be found in our previous chapter. Though acknowledging the difficulty in preparing a forecast without any previous financial records, he showed David that preparing a forecast for the new business was not an impossible task. Let us see what information is needed for the first forecast.

WHAT INFORMATION IS NEEDED FOR THE FIRST FORECAST?

To start a business, you will, of course, need money — your own and/or outside funding. But after financing the start-up costs, the new business must, on its own, generate sufficient profits to support itself and, ideally, to grow. This is the purpose of your first forecast.

Precisely because you don't have a financial history, it is essential that you gather all the information and data that applies to your first year of operation. Finding the answers to the following questions will help give you the information that you need for your first forecast.

Market   Who will your customers be? The type of business you are considering will, in part, determine the answer to this question. If you are thinking of a fishing camp, your market will be the angler. If you want to make widgets, you would need to know who uses them. In the case of the widget manufacturer, for example, additional questions arise from the initial question: Is the market for widgets growing or contracting?

If your widget is superior in say, wearing qualities, a further question might be: "Will a longer-wearing widget be attractive to these customers?" The longer-wearing widget may be of interest to the users. On the other hand, though, you might find that your possible customers are not interested in a longer-wearing widget, since they are more expensive than those they now use, and because the existing type of widget lasts as long as the equipment in which it is used. It might not make sense for prospective customers to purchase a product they do not really need.

Where are the customers located? This may affect your decision on location of the business, advertising, and how many salesmen to employ.

How will the customers order? Will they order regularly or irregularly and will they place a few large orders or several small ones? What will be the frequency of rush orders? Answers to these questions will affect your inventory requirements, the scheduling of production and possibly the number of employees you will require.

Prices   What are the prices of competitive products? Do these include freight costs? Are discounts given by competitive businesses? What price structure do you need in order to make reasonable profits?

Material   What will be the cost of the materials you need? How well established are your suppliers? What is their reputation for quality, service, and delivery?

Competition   Who are your competitors? Are they large or small companies? How are they likely to respond to your company's entry into the widget-making business? Are they likely to reduce the price of their own product, improve service, or develop their own longer-lasting widget in response to your possible threat to their business? How long might it take them to develop such a widget? In other words, how much time do you have to become an established widget supplier? Could you still compete effectively if competitors were to take a run at you? Can they afford to do so? How many widgets can you sell and at what price?

Facilities and Equipment   What kind of facilities do you need? What are the costs of facilities and equipment? What are the relative costs of leasing and purchasing facilities and equipment? Is adequate equipment available? When, and under what conditions (warranty, delivery, etc.) can it be obtained? What are the reputations of the various manufacturers of the equipment?

Employees   What skills will your employees need? If you have decided on a location where you would prefer to establish your business, is there an adequate supply of possible employees with the required skills? Can these skills be readily taught? Is there a training facility in the area or will you have to do the training yourself? What wage rates and benefits will you have to pay? What relationship do other businesses in the area have with their employees? Will you pay by the hour or on some other basis, for example, piecework?

Production Costs   How much will the material to make a widget cost? Is there any difference in material costs for different numbers of

21

widgets produced? What will power cost and how much will be needed to operate your equipment, and heat and light your facilities? How many widgets can an employee produce? How many widgets do you need each employee to produce to sell the volume expected? What regulatory authorities will you have to deal with? What are the regulations you will have to obey? How much will complying with these regulations cost?

Financial   What kind of record-keeping system should you have? Will you need a bookkeeper or a full-time accountant? If you need to borrow money, can it be obtained? What terms will you get?

Working Capital   What inventory level will you need in raw materials and finished products? What is the amount of accounts receivable you can expect to have on your books at any one time? What payment terms would apply? What are the payment terms of your suppliers? How long would it take for the purchased material to be sold as finished products? What proportion of your sales would be for cash or immediate payment? Is additional working capital available if you need it?

These questions are by no means intended to be an exhaustive list. However, having answered them should put you in a better position to prepare your first forecast.

THE FIRST FORECAST

How does the new business with no past financial history prepare its first forecast? As we know, a forecast entails the following calculation:

$$\text{Sales} - \text{Cost of Goods Sold} = \text{Gross Margin}$$
$$\text{Gross Margin} - \text{Operating Expenses} = \text{Profit}$$

Let us look at each calculation individually.

Sales   This is the most important figure to calculate realistically. An error in your estimate of sales, especially if on the high side, could lead you into business without the ability to show a profit.

The new business is translating its estimated share of the market into a dollar figure. Yet, at the same time, this figure must bear a relationship to cost of goods sold. If you are a new manufacturer, your estimate of sales must not exceed your capacity to produce finished products and must take into consideration the time required to actually produce the finished products. In other words, you must first have something to sell.

For the retailer, the ability to purchase inventory must be in direct relationship to the amount of sales and the factor of stock turn-over. For the service business primarily selling a skill, the factor of time must be recognized.

Estimating sales is difficult for the new business. A high priced item means that your sales figure is probably derived by multiplying the number of items you estimate to sell by the selling price. A large variety of products with a low price will mean the sales figure is determined on a volume basis. The selling price itself can be difficult to establish; though in most cases it will have to be primarily based on your competitors' prices and may only marginally reflect your own needs and circumstances.

Cost of Goods Sold Forecasting how much your product costs will naturally depend on how much you intend to sell and what inventory levels you will have. As with sales, if your product is high-priced, your cost of goods sold can be calculated by multiplying the product's cost by the number of items you intend to sell. If your product is low-priced, your cost of goods sold will be calculated in relationship with your inventory levels. For example, you take your beginning inventory and add to it the purchases you intend for that period, and the result is your goods available for sale. When you subtract your ending inventory from goods available for sale, you have your cost of goods sold.

Cost of goods sold will reflect the factors of: time, ability to purchase and carry inventories, stock turn-over, and the ability to manufacture. Again, it is important to stress the relationship of cost of goods sold to sales.

Gross Margin Calculated once you have determined your sales and cost of goods sold.

Operating Expenses Estimating your operating expenses is one of the most difficult things to do when you have no past experience on which to rely. Regardless of how thorough you are in estimating general and administrative expenses, chances are that you will run into more expenses than anticipated. For this reason it is crucial that in the first forecast you calculate a 10 to 15 percent contingency for unaccounted expenses.

Profit   Once you have arrived at an operating expense figure, your profit is calculated by subtracting your operating expenses from your gross margin.

Note: Statistics Canada and other trade associations have available average percentages of cost of goods sold and various expenses for a large number of retail and manufacturing businesses. This can be helpful as a guide in preparing the first forecast.

Your forecast, if realistically done, should indicate if there is enough profit to meet your needs and provide for any scheduled debt repayments. It is important that, if your forecast shows an insufficient profitability, you do not simply revise it. Check that all your estimates are accurate. If they are, you will have to seriously consider the implications of proceeding with your proposed new business or make major modifications if you have just begun.

A first year forecast may look like this:

David Miller
Sports Car Speciality
First year forecast

Sales		$96,000 [1]
Cost of Goods Sold		58,000 [2]
Gross Margin		38,000
Operating Expenses:		
Wages — part-time clerk	$ 8,000	
Salary — owner	10,000 [3]	
Overhead	800 [4]	
Depreciation — fixtures	1,500	
Depreciation — building	1,300	
Garage expenses	3,000 [5]	
Telephone	300	
Interest	1,800 [6]	
Advertising	500	
Bad debt expenses	300	
Business taxes	250	
Realty taxes	400	
Total Operating Expenses		28,150
Profit before Taxes		9,850 [7]

NOTES:

1. *Sales estimated as follows: The garage has two bays equalling three customers a day for a daily average of $500 in sales. To be conservative, the owner allows one day a week to average out as no revenue earnings. Therefore, $8,000 a month is estimated in sales.*

2. *Cost of goods sold includes owner's time as a mechanic and one other full-time mechanic. Mechanics' wages including fringe benefits are $10.00 an hour; therefore, $140 a day. Cost of goods sold also includes cost of parts used in repairs.*

3. Owner draws a salary in addition to the wages he pays himself as a mechanic.
4. Light, heat, and power expenses that are not applicable to the cost of goods sold calculation are shown as overhead. An example of this is the portion of the expenses applicable to the office in the garage.
5. Miscellaneous operating expenses such as consumable supplies not directly attributable to the repair of a customer's car are entered here as garage expenses.
6. A loan was taken out to finance the purchase of the garage and the start-up. This is the interest payable, not the principal.
7. Profit before taxes should not be confused with the actual funds available to the business. Actual funds means profit less estimated income taxes plus depreciation. These actual funds can be used for debit retirement, inventory build-up, etc.

CONCLUSION

At the outset, the new business will always be faced with the risk of failure. The preparation of a forecast will not eliminate this risk. Rather, the forecast can provide some further insight into the possible risks involved and provide you with a more informed basis on which to judge them. It can reduce the number of surprises that might lie ahead for your business.

3. CHANGES OF OWNERSHIP

"The buying and selling of a small business can be a complex process. But careful planning and a clear understanding of the process will lessen the complexity."

— CASE Counsellor

INTRODUCTION

A change in the ownership of a business has all the components of the simplest marketplace activity: a product, a seller, and a potential buyer. But the selling and the buying of a business is also one of the most complex. Why? Because the seller's price tag on a business is usually more than the value of the business's tangible assets — those assets that can be seen and touched. The difference between the price tag and the assets of the business is an intangible commodity called goodwill.

How does the seller put a price tag on this intangible goodwill? How does the buyer know that the evaluation is a true one?

This chapter is about value: the value of a business to the seller, and the value of a business to the buyer. It also examines how the value of a business is determined so that it is agreeable to both parties. Without this agreed value, there can be no go-ahead for a change in ownership.

SELLING A SMALL BUSINESS

Let us assume that you are the owner of a small business that you have built from scratch and, for personal reasons, you wish to sell it. Where do you start?

You start by establishing a price for the business. There is no point in advertising its availability unless you have a price in mind. A ballpark figure will not excite a prospective buyer any more than a price tag on a piece of merchandise that reads, "Between $150 and $200".

1. Setting your price

As a seller, you must forget about your past investment of time and personal money, and base your price on present and future factors. Potential buyers are interested mainly in the ability of the business to yield a fair return on their investment after they have drawn a reasonable salary from its income. They will be interested in the immediate and long-term potential of the business to determine if it will yield a return on investment equal to, if not better than, alternative investments.

If the business has a limited potential for growth, the prospective buyer will not likely offer you more than the value of the tangible assets (those assets that can be touched, weighed, or measured) which could then be resold on a piecemeal basis. The buyer would not ascribe any value to goodwill which, in a very real sense, is directly related to the earning power and potential of the business.

2. How to determine your asking price

You can determine your asking price by proceeding as follows:

(a) Establish the tangible net worth of the business (that is, assets less liabilities, ignoring any intangible assets such as goodwill).

(b) Estimate what dollar return — perhaps 10% — an investor would get on this amount if invested elsewhere with approximately the same degree of risk. This is called earning power.

(c) Add a reasonable salary for the new owner.

(d) Establish from the operating statements the average annual net earnings before taxes (net profit before deducting owner's drawings) for the past few years. This gives a means of comparing the historical earnings with those the prospective buyer could get from alternative sources open to him. The trend of historical earnings is the key factor.

(e) Deduct the earning power (b) plus reasonable salary (c) from the average net earnings (d) to determine the business's extra earning power.

(f) To value the intangibles, multiply (e) by the number of years of profitable operation. A well-established and successful business would justify using a factor of five or more; a less well-based enterprise might suggest a factor of three as appropriate.

(g) Final asking price — tangible net worth (a) plus value of intangibles (f).

Here's how the price formula can be applied to two businesses up for sale.

	Business A	Business B
(a) Tangible net worth	$40,000	$40,000
(b) Earning power — 10% of (a)	4,000	4,000
(c) Reasonable salary for owner	10,000	10,000
(d) Average net earnings	16,000	12,000
(e) Extra earning power		
(d) minus (b) and (c)	2,000	−2,000
(f) Value of intangibles		
(e) times 5	10,000	nil
(g) Final asking price		
(a) plus (f)	$50,000	$40,000

In the case of Business A, the seller should get a substantial price of $10,000 for the intangibles (goodwill) because the business is well established and is probably earning more than the potential buyer would likely get elsewhere with comparable effort and risk. The buyer would, in this example, recover the cost of goodwill (f) in five years. The reasoning is that if the business continues to average $26,000 net earnings per year, the buyer will realize his 10 percent return of $4,000, his salary of $10,000 plus $2,000 extra earnings each year. This last amount would equal, in five years, the $10,000 he paid initially for the goodwill.

For Business B, there is no goodwill value because there is no extra earning power (e) and a prospective buyer might even conclude that the business was not worth its tangible net worth (a) because of the poor return on an investment of that size. Intangible assets often include patents, franchises, organization expenses, and trade marks as well as goodwill.

3. Attracting prospective buyers

Having set a price that you feel reflects the business's present and future value, you can attract prospective buyers in one or more of the following ways:

Word of mouth disclosures Informing your suppliers or business associates might bring you nibbles, but there will be few serious bites unless you know of a party who has previously expressed interest in owning your kind of business.

Classified newspaper advertising This medium is inexpensive and effective providing the ad specifies price, location, size of business, and potential sales volume. You should decide in advance if you wish ir - quiries to be made by telephone or mail.

Real estate brokers Though you must pay them a commission they have their finger on the pulse of the market. They will screen prospective buyers and will ensure that all the proper legal steps are taken.

Trade publications These are effective in reaching prospects already active in the kind of business you are selling.

4. Prepare your sales pitch (in writing)

To illustrate why you as a seller should be prepared, let us look at the following story:

Glen Harvey, after almost twenty-three years in business, decided to sell his hardware store. It was a difficult decision but the reasons were personal and involved his only son who had decided neither to work in the store nor to become a partner. So Glen placed a number of ads in the papers, and waited.

The first serious enquiry that Glen received went something like this:

"You're asking $110,000 for the shop?" questioned the man holding the newspaper. "I think that's high."

"Oh no," countered Glen. "There's a lot of business done from this shop. I've really established a good clientele."

"Can you prove it?"

Glen produced a set of financial statements.

"These are last year's statements," observed the enquirer. "Plus this is just the balance sheet. I want to see current operating statements plus statements for as many years back as possible."

Glen scratched his head. "I'll have to see my accountant. But in the meantime look around the place."

The man asked Glen a lot more questions and Glen found himself constantly saying that he'd get the figures or speak to his accountant. The enquirer was constantly asking for proof and was belittling the price that Glen was asking. He even expressed disbelief at Glen's answer of personal reasons for selling.

"I might be back," announced the enquirer. "But there are a couple of other places I want to look at first."

The door closed on Glen. He was perplexed. He knew the price was a fair one but how was he to prove it?

Just as Glen advertises and promotes his products, he should do the same when selling his business. Serious prospective buyers will ask for written documentation describing a business's past performance, present level of business activity, and future growth prospects.

The package of material that should be assembled should include:

- a brief history of the business from its incorporation to the present, and an estimate of its growth potential

- balance sheets and operating statements for the previous years, and an interim statement

- a written statement setting out the basis of establishing and evaluating the asking price

BUYING A BUSINESS

So you have weighed the pros and cons between starting a business from scratch and buying an existing one, and have decided to buy. Where do you begin?

The same methods that the seller uses can be your starting point:

Word-of-mouth disclosures   People such as suppliers, bankers, Board of Trade members may tell you about particular owners who are thinking of selling. Further enquiry might prove such disclosures to be rumours, but it could lead to a genuine prospect.

Classified newspaper ads   They give a capsule description of the kind of business that is for sale, the reason for sale, and often a ballpark price that represents a point from which you can negotiate. Steer clear of ads that promise "fabulous profits to be made in the fastest growing business in the '80s" or "once in a lifetime opportunity to cash in on the bonanza." If such businesses really do yield fabulous profits, they don't need this kind of flamboyant advertising.

Real estate brokers   When describing a business for sale, brokers will tell you more about the tangibles such as the plant and equipment, than about the intangibles. But through them you can arrange to visit the current owners.

Trade publications   These can be ideal for finding out which businesses are for sale and where they are located. One drawback is that because of the time it takes to publish, advertisements are often for businesses that were sold just prior to, or just following the publication's release.

1. Contacting the seller

If you see an advertisement for a business that appears attractive as an investment, or you hear of such a business that is about to be put onto the market, make your first contact with the owner by telephone. Ask questions that elicit information such as "If you had the capital, how would you expand your business?" If the owner sounds doubtful about the business's potential for growth, ask why. You should know. Jot down all the information the owner reveals about the business, then arrange for an appointment. Before the meeting, visit competitors, check available products and prices, check suppliers' prices, and visit the business incognito to get a feel for the premises especially if it is a restaurant or a shop. Pretend you are a customer and note the morale of the employees. When you pay a formal visit, ask the owner to provide you with documentation, such as financial statements, photocopies of the lease if the business is in leased premises, and sales promotion brochures describing the business's products or services.

2. Verifying the information

If there are trouble spots in the business, the seller is not going to alert you to them. Like a doctor examining a patient, you must examine the business to determine its state of health.

Carefully check the following:

The owner's reason for selling   The seller might want to retire, but why? Is this because he or she is near retirement age, or is it because the demand of the business on the owner's time and energies is exhausting? Find out.

The seller's financial statements and records   They may indicate the owner's real reason for selling. Verify them against tax returns.

Operating documentation   This includes the calculation of costs of goods sold, sales, and operating expenses. It also entails the pricing structure and rate of inventory turnover. You can check some of this data with suppliers. Compare productivity with similar businesses. Confirm prices and sales patterns.

The value of the tangibles   This means the equipment, premises, and inventory. Compare their value with the costs of starting from scratch.

The value of the intangibles   Can the monetary value that the seller applies to the intangible assets — the business's reputation, regular clientele, and potential for earning a better than average profit — be justified?

General conditions   Get a feel for employee morale, the bustle created by customers and the competition. Are there too many businesses competing for a diminishing market? Is the surrounding area becoming more or less prosperous? Do government regulations help or hinder you in the kind of business you wish to enter?

If in doubt about certain results of your research, consult an expert. Better to pay a little for good advice than to pay a lot for your bad judgment.

3. The asking price — if high, why?

The seller is entitled to set an asking price that allows room for manoeuvre once bargaining begins. Why might an asking price seem unreasonably high? There can be a number of reasons such as:

- The current owner includes his or her salary in profits, or draws an unrealistically low salary for time and skills input, thereby inflating profits.
- The owner doesn't pay interest on the capital that he or she has put into the business. This inflates profits.
- The current owner doesn't worry as much about future risk as the potential owner.
- The current owner has an emotional attachment to the business. The evaluation is based on a distorted sense of the business's reputation among its clients.
- The current owner needs the amount of the asking price to finance the planned retirement or next business venture.
- The current owner has been led to expect a high offer by an enthusiastic broker looking for a listing, by reports of other business sales, or by encouragement from family members.
- The current owner wishes to recoup the losses in time and money put into the business in its first years of growth.
- The current owner's asking price is based on a too optimistic earning potential. "Population is due to double in the next five years", the owner might assure you. That might be true; but the competition, property assessments, and taxes may also double.

If the asking price seems unreasonably low, don't dismiss it as a losing proposition. It could be a genuine bargain if:

- Earnings have been low due to poor management that you can rectify.

- The current owner **has** to sell. A due to illness sale could mean just that.

- You can get improved economies of operation by combining the business with another venture.

- The owner fails to appreciate the true value of the business, perhaps due to valuing assets at their original cost or even the depreciated book value.

- The alternative of starting from scratch is not as feasible due to present market conditions.

4. Measuring a business's profit

The owner of a business can receive financial benefits from his or her business in three major ways: by earning interest on a personal loan to the business, by drawing a salary, and by earning a profit. How do these three ways affect the goodwill?

Interest   The owner may loan money to the business rather than borrow at a bank. If so, the owner should receive interest on these loans, equivalent to prevailing rates. This is an expense, and will reduce true profit. Owners who make low interest or interest-free loans give the business a false profit picture.

Salary   The owner who works for the business should draw a fair salary and range of benefits. These are expenses which will reduce the profit figure. Often owners don't draw a fair salary for the time and energy they put into the business, or pay salaries to their relatives who help in the business. Then there are owners who pay themselves too much and claim expenses which are really personal benefits. This gives an equally false profit picture to a business. It is up to you to discern the real salary.

Profit   This is what is left over after deducting expenses (including the owner's salary), and it can be the most arbitrary of the three owner's earnings. Here are three examples of just how arbitrary it can be.

Tom loans the business his own $20,000 with no interest charges, and pays himself a nominal salary. Dick borrows his $20,000 from a bank and draws a fair salary for his role. Harriette draws as much as she can in salary, borrows $30,000 from the bank so she can buy a car for her personal use, and pays for travel and entertainment expenses through the business.

	Tom	Dick	Harriette
Revenue of business	$100,000	$100,000	$100,000
Salary	12,000	20,000	24,000
Bank Interest	nil	2,500	3,600
Other Expenses	70,000	70,000	79,400
Profit or (Loss)	$ 18,000	$ 7,500	$ (7,000)

Is Tom's business really more profitable and hence worth more? No, he is just understating his true expenses. He should pay himself interest on the loan and draw a more realistic salary. Is Harriette's business really a losing operation? No, she's just using it to pay for lifestyle benefits that she hasn't earned.

Note that all three businesses are the same, but profit is calculated in three different ways.

Profits for the immediate future should also be considered. One expense that is often ignored is depreciation on capital assets. This is particularly important if the seller wants to sell you the assets at more than their book value. You will have to claim a higher depreciation expense, thus reducing profit. Also check for major expense increases such as rent, insurance, renegotiated equipment leases, etc., which will affect the profit picture in the coming year.

5. The business's worth from the buyer's perspective

Just as the seller has assigned a dollar value to the tangible and intangible assets of the business, you must also do the same. Estimate the value of:

Equipment and furniture Major items should be valued at the going market price for used equipment in similar condition, less a fraction to allow for the fact that they would be sold as a bulk lot.

Supplies and small items   Some supplies are virtually unsalable except to the buyer of the business, and therefore have little value. These would include open containers of supplies, printed stationery, Christmas decorations, and similar.

Inventory   Inventory is generally valued at cost except for old stock which has not moved well, or has become outdated and will therefore sell for even less. You should not pay for unsalable items. Consider using the services of an independent appraiser to arrive at an objective estimate.

Leasehold improvements   If the seller has made necessary improvements to the premises or site which are not reflected in the rent, this has some value, but you must write it off as an expense during the duration of the current lease. But don't allow for the entire cost of the improvement because the vendor hasn't the choice of selling the improvements to a party other than the buyer of the business.

Accounts receivable   As a rule, the buyer doesn't take these over. But if you agree to, discount them to allow for the risk of possible bad debts and the cost of financing. A simple listing of these accounts by age can help you determine what they are worth.

Goodwill   In one sense, goodwill includes the intangibles such as the business's reputation and regular clientele. In another sense, it is the ability of a business to earn better than average profits. It can be the result of good management, an excellent location, a special process, or a patent, etc. If the business earns more than the 12 or 15 percent that you could expect to earn on another investment, then you will likely have to pay a premium to buy this earning power. That is what you buy when you pay for goodwill.

Goodwill is measured in multiples of true profits. Whether you use a small multiple or a large one depends mainly on the element of risk you expect. A long-established business with stable earning power might sell for a low one. Basically, the multiple reflects how quickly you want your investment repaid. The greater the risk, the quicker you want your money back.

Totalling the preceding six items will give you an approximate estimate of the worth of the business. Let the total represent your final price offer. Initially offer less. A business is worth no more than the highest price someone will pay, and no less than the lowest price the seller will accept.

6. Negotiating the sale

The handshake price isn't the only negotiable item when buying a business. You negotiate a package deal which could include:

Vendor financing   The seller might provide financing. If so, agree to terms such as the down payment, interest rate, duration, and collateral.

Pre-disposition of certain assets   If you don't want the company car included in the deal, ask the seller to dispose of it in a separate sale to another buyer.

Price allocation for tax purposes   As a buyer, you will want the highest possible expense amount (fees, interest, supplies, inventory); the highest possible valuation of depreciable assets (equipment, small tools, leasehold improvements); and as little as possible for goodwill. The seller will want the opposite.

Fees to the seller   The seller might ask for a consulting fee during the change-over, or a percentage of future income.

Noncompetitive agreement   The goodwill you pay for will count for nothing if the owner sets up a new business across the street and takes away the customer base that comes with the business. Draw up an agreement to ensure that if the former owner does set up another business, it will be remote from yours.

Before entering into negotiations, consider these factors, and be prepared to trade some of them for concessions you will want from the seller.

7. Concessions you can offer

As part of the purchase package, you might offer some concessions which might appeal to the seller, yet be advantageous to you. They could include:

- An agreement to work for the seller for one month prior to the change-over. For this free or minimal paid labour, you will get invaluable training.

- A higher offer if granted a lower interest rate or other favourable financing terms.

- Paying consulting fees for a year or two as part of the price. This is, in fact, an interest-free, unsecured loan to you. You can write it off as a full expense. For the seller, it might spread the taxable gains over several years.

- Repayment in the form of balloon payments. These are large amounts paid at annual periods rather than monthly.

- A percentage of next year's gross as part of the price, up to a specified limit. The seller has the hope of getting more if the business does, in fact, have excellent growth prospects. You are protected in case things don't go well. It's also an interest-free loan.

- Pay part of the price as a consulting fee to a relative whose income tax bracket is lower than that of the seller.

- Pay the seller a commission for a year on any new accounts that he or she brings in. Give a discount to the seller on personal purchases.

8. Making your offer

Before you sign an offer, protect yourself with the inclusion of some escape clauses, usually referred to as subject clauses, such as:

- subject to buyer obtaining financing on satisfactory terms

- subject to vendor making all records available to buyer and/or accountant for full inspection and verification

- subject to buyer's lawyer approving the terms and form of agreement

- subject to buyer having the opportunity to view operations in detail, and time to verify and supplement information presented to date

- subject to buyer receiving necessary licenses, permits, registrations, etc., including use of existing premises as is (i.e. no improvements required to satisfy health codes, etc.)
- subject to property owner approving sublease to buyer
- subject to equipment, leases, debts, etc., being transferred to buyer

You should keep these subject clauses general. They usually have a time limit during which you must remove them or else the agreement becomes invalid.

Your offer should also allow for price adjustments for items likely to change before you assume ownership. This would include a reduction or increases if the inventory is different from that noted in the seller's list of current assets. Set a maximum figure for such items. Adjustments for expenses prepaid by the vendor or for income received in advance, such as deposits, should also be included.

CONCLUSION

Setting a value on a business is the major problem encountered when the ownership of a business is about to be changed. There are two values inherent in the same business: the value to the seller, and the value to the buyer.

The value of the tangible assets can be mutually agreed to because they are measurable by objective standards. The value of the intangibles, mainly goodwill, is subjective. But to allow a change of ownership to take place, there must be an agreement between the seller and the buyer as to both values.

4. PRESENTING YOUR CASE FOR A TERM LOAN

"Regardless of where you seek term financing, each lender will require basically the same information."

— CASE Counsellor

INTRODUCTION

What information would you want to know if you were asked to lend your money to someone for several years? Probably quite a lot for you would want to be sure that your money would not only earn interest but that it would be a safe investment. So when your business needs a term loan, remember that you, too, will be asked for information. This information constitutes presenting a case for a term loan.

This chapter introduces you to the concept of term financing. It looks at the need for presenting a viable case for a loan, and, as well, examines what information and paperwork a lender will want.

WHAT IS TERM FINANCING?

Term financing is a definition used to describe the borrowing of money in which the repayment takes place within a certain period of time, or term. Term financing, or debt financing as it is sometimes called, is often defined by its terms of repayment: **short-term**, **intermediate-term**, and **long-term**.

Short-term financing Generally extended to a business for one year or less. These loans are obtained to meet working capital needs such as operating expenses, seasonal slack periods, and inventory build-ups. Short-term loans may also be used for an interim period while arranging longer term financing.

Intermediate-term financing Used for periods of more than one year but usually for less than five years. This financing provides monies for other than temporary needs. These needs can include the starting of a new business, the buying of an existing one, the expansion of operations, the purchase of assets, or for leasehold improvements.

Long-term financing Financing for a period exceeding five years. Usually, the purpose of the loan is to purchase a high value asset such as a building or land.

In defining a term loan, it is important to know that this type of financing has particular characteristics:

- the interest rate at time of borrowing is slightly higher than other types of loans
- normally there is a fixed interest rate for a specific period of time — payments stay the same
- often, the loan is secured by fixed assets
- time length of loan is specific and agreed upon
- the loan may take time to obtain

WHY PRESENT A CASE FOR A TERM LOAN?

Before examining the information and the accompanying paperwork that a lender will require, it can be helpful to really understand the need for presenting your case for a term loan. Let us look at the following situation:

"Well, do you at least have an idea of how much money you need?" asked the loan officer.

"Oh yes," replied Paul. "We need $45,000."

"Yes, that's the amount," interrupted Paul's partner Eric. "But to that figure you must add $12,000 for buying the used tow truck."

"Just a moment now," said the loan officer. "The two of you, as partners, want to open a service station, right?"

"That's it," said Paul, "and we need a loan to get started. We can put up almost $15,000 cash of our own money."

"Is that $15,000 part of your $45,000, or rather $57,000, requirement?" asked the loan officer.

"We're using the $15,000," replied Eric. "The $57,000 is the money we still need."

"Have you thought about how you will pay back the loan?"

"Yes," answered Paul. "We should be able to manage the payments."

"But what about your other debts? Listen, you say you have a great idea for a business but you can't expect to get financing by just saying that you have a good idea. There's information and paperwork that I need. This can be summarized as knowing: who you are, what you plan to do, and what will happen once you get the loan.

"I want to know your financial background to see if there's any additional financial support in case your business gets in trouble. I need financial statements for your proposed first year in business.

"This will show me the anticipated operation, your anticipated sales and profits, and why you need the loan.

"I also need a cash flow for your first 12 months. This shows if the loan amount is justified and if you will have any problems in meeting your operating debt and also paying back the loan. Then, there is the question of security..."

"Wait," interjected Paul. "Do you really need all that information?"

"Yes — you must not only prove to me that any money I invest in your business will earn interest and be safe, you must also prove it to yourself that you can make a go of it."

A well thought out and prepared presentation will go a long way in helping both the new and existing business sell itself for a term loan. Remember, the supply of money can be tight at times and, at all times, you are in competition for the same financing monies.

WHAT DOES A LENDER WANT TO KNOW?

The purpose of our story about Paul and Eric was to illustrate why a lender needs information and paperwork. The question that next follows is what information will the lender need when considering your presentation for a term loan.

The loan officer in our story summarized the information as: **who you are**, **what you plan to do**, and **what will happen once you get the loan**. As well, he added the aspects of **security** and **financial strength**.

1. Who you are

This question applies not only to yourself as the owner but also to the business itself. The quality of management in your business is of utmost importance. Explaining who you are gives the term lender an idea of what to expect from the management of your business. Of interest to the lender is: your education, your experience (or lack of it), your accomplishments, your shortcomings and who on your management team can compensate for them. Write these facts down. Term lenders can also compare, from their own experience, the relative strengths of your management with many other businesses, particularly those in your industry. Obviously your diligence and determination to be a success will also be major factors. No management group in a small business is likely to appear perfect to an outsider. Discussing your business with a term lender may sometimes lead you to make improvements in your organization that may eliminate possible future problems.

Of greatest single importance to most lenders, and naturally to you, is the ability of your business to earn sufficient profits to repay the term loan, with enough remaining funds to meet the normal needs of the business. Without this ability your business will fail. It is for this reason that financial statements are required by the lender so as to demonstrate that your venture is viable.

To complete the picture of you and your business, the lender will also ask for non-financial details of your enterprise such as the history of the business, its growth potential, as well as details of operations and products.

2. What you plan to do

To show a term lender what you plan to do, demonstrate your plan and its financing, in the following way:

PROGRAMME

Purchase land	$11,000
Construct building addition	50,000
Purchase & install equipment	17,000
Provision for contingencies	8,000
	$86,000

FINANCING

Term loan	$59,000
Additional shareholders' investment	27,000
	$86,000

This simple presentation can then be expanded with footnotes or attached sheets, giving the details of each item, for example: the size, location and legal description of the land, and the plans for the building addition.

You should indicate clearly which items of the cost are firm, and which are only based on estimates. In the above example, a provision for contingencies of $8,000 is included to allow for such things as inaccuracies in estimating, items overlooked, and changes during construction that may involve extra cost. The amount that you should provide for contingencies depends on the nature of your programme and the portion which is subject to estimates. Even for the portion which is firm, there will often be changes made while the programme is in progress, particularly where it involves the installation of machinery and equipment. These changes often add to the cost of the programme. In some cases, a contingency reserve of at least 50 percent is desirable even when a large part of the programme is covered by firm commitments. In the average case, a cost overrun of 10 percent to 20 percent can be expected. A corresponding provision for contingencies at the outset will prevent a shortage of funds when your programme is only partially completed.

It is also important to demonstrate to the term lender that your programme will bring tangible benefits to your business. In the case of a large sophisticated business, with careful control over capital budgeting, it is normal for a lender to require that an analysis be made of what is expected from a particular project by way of decreased costs and increased net revenues. For a small business, without the same degree of sophistication in capital budgeting, such an analysis is difficult to prepare. In any case, there should be some thought given to the potential savings to be derived from the programme. If the main purpose of the programme is physical expansion to take care of increasing sales volume, you must ensure that the expansion is in reasonable relation to the expected sales volume, as there are few businesses that can really afford to have a large amount of unused or excess capacity.

Finally, you must show details of how you propose to finance your programme. Sometimes this will simply be the term loan. In other cases, the programme might involve additional investment by you, or perhaps the use of working capital. In the case of additional investment, a lender will normally want to be assured that this money is available. If part of the financing is to come from working capital, it is helpful to have prepared an analysis of how this can be accomplished without jeopardizing the working capital required for the normal day-to-day financing of the business.

3. What will happen once you get the loan?

The answer to this question is the justification for requesting the term loan in the first place. This is when the term lender will want to know what your financial situation will be like in the future. You will probably have more assets purchased with the new financing. You will also have more liabilities, including the term loan, and perhaps there will be a new investment by you and others.

The lender will analyze your financial future by requesting a pro-forma balance sheet, profit and loss statement, and cash flow. These statements of the future will be examined to ensure that the amount of new debt will not upset the balance of total debt to owners' investment that a successful business should maintain. They will also show what the business will earn in the years following completion of your plan. In other words, these future or pro-forma financial statements must show that a term loan is needed, that it can be paid back, and that in getting the loan a definite benefit will be derived by the business.

4. Security

Since most term loans are secured by the term lender taking a charge on the fixed assets of the business, it is apparent that the security value of these assets is also a criterion affecting the amount of term financing you might obtain. If the fixed assets of your business comprise only leasehold improvements, which usually have a very low relative recovery value in the event of liquidation, it is obvious that security values would be very low. On the other hand, a mortgage on a well-located, general purpose building of good quality construction, represents very good security. However, many lenders are prepared to make a loan which is under-secured by the fixed assets if the business has excellent earning prospects. Be prepared to describe your land, buildings, machinery, and equipment.

5. Financial strength

Finally, there is the general financial strength of the business now and after your plan is completed. Will there be sufficient capital to meet trade debts promptly, to survive seasonal lulls comfortably, and to maintain good deliveries and service to your customers? Again your balance sheets and profit and loss statements will enable the term lender to make a few simple tests to be ensured of your financial strength.

From this brief introduction on what information is needed by a term lender, we shall next look in detail at the form in which this information should be presented to the term lender.

WHAT PAPERWORK MAY BE REQUESTED

You will know what your business is all about but the lender will, of course, not know it in the same detail. The lender may even know nothing at all about your business. Because it is to your advantage to prove to the lender that a loan for your business is a wise and safe transaction, you will want to sell yourself in the best manner possible.

The best manner possible means a presentation that is clear, straightforward, and is in a format that can be both examined and referred to again. Naturally, this means paperwork.

Let us look at what paperwork is usually required when presenting your case for a term loan. Not all this paperwork may be requested by every lender, but it is a good idea to know what to expect.

Resume of the principals Give a brief background of the owners and key people who work, or will work, in the business. Emphasize why they are valuable to the business. This information allows the lender to assess management abilities.

Resume of the business Describe the basic non-financial background of the business. In other words, include such facts as: when the business was started, who started it, why it was started, where it was started, the legal structure, operating and product details, major suppliers, customers, and the advantages the business has over other concerns. In short, this tells the lender what the business is all about.

Personal financial statements Often required for a new business situation, especially if the principals have never been in business before. A personal financial statement will show the lender what additional financing is available to the business should it get into financial difficulties.

Financial statements These include a profit and loss statement, a balance sheet, and a statement of retained earnings. For an existing business, these statements should be for the last five years or, if less than five years, for as many years as is possible. For a new business with no financial history, statements should be prepared for the proposed first year of operation. This information permits the lender to analyze the financial situation of the business (assets, liabilities, growth, equity, and short-falls). It allows the lender to assess the worth of the business.

Profit and loss statement for the future   Statements to be done for both the current year and for the following twelve-month period. This tells the lender what the future will be for the business and if the loan can be repaid.

Cash flow for the future   Done for a twelve-month period and includes the proceeds of the requested loan. This shows the lender why the loan is needed and where any problems in repayment may occur.

List of securable assets   Useful to the lender if the term loan must be secured. A simple list of available fixed or movable assets should include descriptions of the assets, when they were bought, and the purchase price.

Leases, mortgages, insurance policies   If the premises are rented, a copy of the lease will show the lender if the business is liable for any penalties in case of default, or is governed by any restrictions from the lessor. Property owned by the business or owner(s) is a major security item. A copy of the mortgage along with evidence of what principal and interest has been paid and details of any liens will be of interest to the lender.

In preparing the paperwork for presenting a case for a term loan, accuracy is crucial. This is especially true in preparing financial statements, forecasts, and a cash flow. You may wish to consider qualified help at this stage. Qualified help should not only assist you in your preparation, it should also ensure that you fully understand your proposal for a term loan.

CONCLUSION

The information and paperwork that need to be presented to a term lender can be rather imposing. Naturally, if the risk and the amount of the loan is small, the lender's analysis of your presentation need not be as detailed as it would be for a larger loan. The depth of the analysis also depends on the complexity of your business organization, the risk inherent in the particular industry, and many other features. However, the lender cannot make a valid decision on a term loan without considering all these features to some degree. Therefore, being prepared with a well thought out presentation for a term loan will go a long way in proving to the lender, and yourself, that a loan to your business is a good proposition. And remember, if you receive assistance in the preparation of your financial presentation, be sure to understand it as well as possible so as to be able to discuss it intelligently with the lender. This, too, is part of the professionalism required in presenting your case for a term loan.

5. Working Capital

"Working capital is more than the arithmetical difference between current assets and liabilities. It is a reflection of good management if the level is proper for your business."

— *CASE Counsellor*

INTRODUCTION

Expressed in simple terms, working capital is the difference between a business's current assets and its current liabilities. This can be shown by the following equation:

Current Assets − Current Liabilities = Working Capital

Expressed in another way, it is the amount of working (or current) assets such as cash, inventory, receivables which are **not** being financed by current liabilities such as trade credit (accounts payable) or short-term bank credit.

Working capital is an important indicator of a business's liquidity. It should be sufficient to provide for the payment of current liabilities as they come due, and for the financing of day-to-day operations.

Two typical small businesses will be profiled in this chapter to illustrate the influence of working capital on day-to-day operations, and the influence of those same operations on the business's working capital position.

THE FUNCTION OF WORKING CAPITAL

Understanding the function of working capital requires an understanding of the relationship between current assets and current liabilities.

Current liabilities are debts which have to be paid in the near future, normally within twelve months. They are paid by the normal circulation of cash through the business. This circulation results from converting cash to inventories to accounts receivable and back to cash. In the case of cash sales, the cycle is even shorter: cash to inventories and back to cash when a sale is made. Because of the mark-up of the inventory, and of the service sometimes sold with the inventory, the amount of cash received from a sale should be greater than the amount spent on the inventory. Therefore, current assets pay for current liabilities.

The ability of a business to pay its current debts on time depends on the amount and timing of this cash circulation from one type of current asset to another: cash to inventory to receivables to cash to inventory, etc. If this circulation is fast compared to the time available for payment of accounts payable owing to suppliers, the business will have cash to pay its debts on time and will have only a minimum of current assets on hand. In reality, most businesses require a working capital surplus, in other words, more current assets than current liabilities. This is because of the need for large, varied inventories which will probably include slow-moving items. Another reason for a working capital surplus is that many businesses offer credit to their customers, which means carrying accounts receivable.

HOW MUCH WORKING CAPITAL?

How much working capital does a small business need?

The amount of working capital any business needs is determined by:

- the size and kind of inventory it buys (e.g. large and fast-moving such as that of a grocery store, or small and slow-moving like that of an haute couture fashion boutique)
- the amount and terms of its accounts receivable and accounts payable

The above two factors are relative to the business's operating cycle.

There are some analysts who claim that for a business to be truly healthy, it should show a ratio of 2:1 between its current assets and current liabilities. They contend that the need for the amount of current assets to remain at least double the amount of current liabilities is due to the possibilities of shrinkage in the current assets, notably in stated totals for inventories of materials or merchandise. Even if inventories represent sound value, these analysts claim that the inventory will not realize the amount attributed to it in the event of a bulk sale or liquidation.

Ratios, however, are useful only when compared with a reference point. The business owner could compare this year's current asset to current liability ratio with previous years', or with those of other businesses **in the same line**. Comparisons with businesses in other lines are misleading, and could give the owner undue cause for alarm.

In practical terms, a small business should have enough working capital to maintain good purchasing power so that it can buy its inventory requirements and essential services on the best of terms. Adequate working capital enables a business to take advantage of trade discounts when available, and to keep its costs and prices competitive. The owner who maintains a strong working capital position can insist on prompt delivery of inventory supplies and thus avoid stock shortages or over-stocking. The owner, not the creditors, will be able to direct the business; and its credit reputation will remain high.

WORKING CAPITAL AT WORK

To illustrate what working capital means, our next sections deal with two small businesses: Leduc Cleaners owned by Bob Leduc, and Drew Drugs owned by Debbie Drew.

Bob Leduc looked at the papers his accountant had just sent him. One sheet, marked Schedule 2, puzzled him. The heading read "Changes in Working Capital between April 1, 1979 and March 31, 1980."

Bob was a dry cleaner and a good businessman. While he had proven his managerial competence by running his dry cleaning shop profitably for nine years, Bob knew he was no accountant. Working capital was a term without much meaning. He had heard his good friend, Debra Drew, talk about it. Debbie ran the drugstore next door. Maybe druggists learned about working capital at college. Occasionally Debbie grumbled that she was short of working capital, even though her busy store never seemed short of anything.

Bob turned back a page. The top of it read:

LEDUC CLEANERS
Balance Sheet as at March 31st, 1980

ASSETS		LIABILITIES	
Cash	$ 100	Bank advances	$ 3,000
Accounts receivable	500	Accounts payable	5,000
Materials & supplies, at cost	800	Mortgage — current instalments	3,000
Total current assets	$1,400	Total current liabilities	$11,000

This seemed easy enough to follow. All of Bob's customers paid for their cleaning with cash, except the supermarket. Their account for dry cleaning of uniforms was the only account receivable. The inventory of materials and supplies was all there in the shop: cleaning materials, rolls of plastic, hangers, labels, cartons. This was not much in the way of current assets, but it was everything that he needed.

Bob's business had a $5,000 line of credit from the chartered bank down the street. He only used it at certain times during each year and his borrowings had never reached $5,000. So the $3,000 owing to the bank was no problem. Accounts payable of $5,000 looked a little high. Bob decided to have a closer look at that one later. He next looked at the mortgage entry. The $3,000 was a year's payments on his 10-year loan for new equipment. The loan was originally for $30,000. There wasn't much he could do about that.

Bob went back to his accounts payable. He knew that he had grossed $150,000 for the year, or an average of $12,500 per month. He also knew that his purchases of materials and supplies normally amounted to about 10 percent of his revenues. To sell $12,500 in a month, he would have had to buy $1,250 of materials and supplies. The accounts payable figure of $5,000 on the balance sheet would therefore be about four months' purchases. All of his suppliers gave him 30-day terms, so he must be behind in paying some of them. Or could it be that his monthly sales in February and March had been well above the $12,500 average, requiring heavier purchasing? Or were accounts included that were not materials and supplies?

After checking his monthly sales figures and his list of accounts payable at March 31st, Bob found the answer. Sales were $12,900 in February and $11,800 in March. Nothing abnormal about that. But in the accounts payable list all items were materials and supplies, except one, a bill for $3,800 from Grant Electric for his new outdoor sign and new lighting system in the shop. Unpaid bills for normal purchases of materials and supplies were therefore only $1,200 of the $5,000 accounts payable. This was in line with the 30-day terms available.

Debra Drew, the druggist, had said that working capital was the difference between current assets and current liabilities, and that she liked to have twice as many current assets as current liabilities in her drugstore business. She had also said that she had trouble in achieving this.

Bob thought about his own situation. He had just convinced himself that his own current assets and current liabilities were in pretty fair shape. But the current liabilities of $11,000 were far greater than the current assets of $1,400. Leduc Cleaners had a working capital deficit rather than a surplus. Yet nothing seemed wrong. Could it be that each business has its own special requirements for working capital?

Yes. A business, such as Leduc Cleaners, with a high proportion of cash sales, and with credit terms for its purchases, will often have current liabilities greater than its current assets.

Let us take a simple example. Suppose Bob Leduc buys 100 coat hangers. He receives them, along with the invoice specifying 30-day terms, on a Monday. By Friday of the same week, they have all been sold as part of his dry cleaning service, and he has been paid in cash. He doesn't have to pay for the hangers for another 26 days so he has cash available to pay other bills. He can order more hangers or other supplies and receive cash for them from his customers, and then pay for the first 100 hangers. He has no need for large accumulations of cash, supplies or other current assets in order to pay his bills on time. He needs only a small amount of working capital.

That is why working capital means more than just the arithmetical difference between current assets and current liabilities to the person managing a business. **It is really a reflection of the health of each current asset and each current liability under the operating conditions that exist in that business, and none other**. The amount of working capital needed in a business is that which results from each current asset and each current liability being at a manageable level. An example of this is no overdue accounts payable.

As we have said previously, most businesses require a working capital surplus; more current assets than current liabilities. The amounts of these current assets and liabilities and the timing of the operating cycle in each business will determine how much working capital is needed. The small business operator also needs to know what constitutes a manageable or comfortable level for each current asset and liability in his or her business.

ESTIMATING WORKING CAPITAL NEEDS

Bob Leduc was right. The working capital deficit shown on his March 31st balance sheet was satisfactory for his business at its present sales volume. It provided for payment of current debts as they fell due and it provided for the necessary supplies to do business efficiently.

If Bob had tried to predict in January what working capital he should have by March 31st for a sales volume of about $12,500 a month, he probably would have estimated as follows:

CASH (nominal balance)	$ 100	BANK ADVANCES (half of full line of credit)	$ 2,500
ACCOUNTS RECEIVABLE (1 month's billing to supermarket)	500	ACCOUNTS PAYABLE (30 days' purchases)	1,250
MATERIALS & SUPPLIES (for 15 days, based on purchases of $1,250 per month)	625	PAYABLE — Grant Electric	3,800
		Mortgage — Current	3,000
TOTAL CURRENT ASSETS	$ 1,225	TOTAL CURRENT LIABILITIES	$10,550

This estimate would have shown him that a working capital deficit of $9,325 would be satisfactory, with each current item at a tolerable level for the business and its creditors. The figures in the estimate are very close to those which actually existed at March 31st as previously shown.

Estimating the working capital requirements of a business requires estimating a workable amount for each current asset and current liability for that business. To make a meaningful estimate requires answers to the following questions:

1. What cash balance is necessary to cover day-to-day needs?
2. What are the receivables normally composed of and what is their likely recovery pattern, in relation to monthly sales? How many days' sales will normally be awaiting payment?
3. What inventories are required to assure uninterrupted operations at the expected volume of business?
4. What bank credit is available?
5. What terms are available from suppliers and what purchases will be needed on these terms at the expected sales volume?
6. Are there any other current liabilities of significant amounts that will become due during the period considered? An example would be mortgage or lien payments and, in Bob's case, the bill for $3,800 from Grant Electric.

WHAT IF SALES INCREASE?

Many profitable businesses find their progress hampered at times because of a shortage of working capital. Their purchasing power diminishes and their credit reputation may even be affected because they cannot pay their bills on time in accordance with the terms available from their suppliers. This sometimes occurs with businesses experiencing a steady growth in sales, when additional working capital has not been provided to support a higher sales volume. When do sales volumes change so as to affect the required level of working capital?

Changes in sales volume may occur throughout the seasons of every year without a significant change in annual sales. The other situation is a significant increase in annual sales due to an overall expansion of business. Both situations warrant careful consideration of working capital requirements. These two situations can be illustrated by Drew Drugs.

Let us first consider the working capital needs of Drew Drugs as a seasonal business in which monthly sales vary quite widely during a normal 12-month business year. The critical period will be the peak sales period, the months when accounts receivable and inventories will be highest and support from bank borrowings and suppliers will be heavy est.

Debra Drew's drugstore had sales of about $240,000 in each of the past three years. That is an average of about $20,000 per month. In each of those years, her December sales were highest at about $30,000. At June 30th, 1980, her balance sheet showed:

DREW DRUGS
Balance Sheet as at June 30th, 1980

ASSETS		LIABILITIES	
Cash	$ 500	Bank advances	$ 5,000
Accounts receivable	4,000	Accounts payable	25,000
Inventory	40,000		
Total current assets	$44,500	Total current liabilities	$30,000

Sales in June were $20,000 and Debra found this situation quite workable. But what working capital would she need next December? She always seemed short at that time each year.

Debra decided to estimate what her current assets and current liabilities would be at December 31st.

At June 30th, her business had $14,500 of working capital, as shown above. She drew up an estimate of her balance sheet (current portion) for December 31st, 1980, based on a $30,000 sales level, as follows:

CASH	$ 500	BANK ADVANCES (limit of her credit)	$ 7,000
RECEIVABLES (50% more than June 30th)	6,000	ACCOUNTS PAYABLE (50% more than June 30th)	37,500
INVENTORY (50% more than June 30th)	60,000		
TOTAL CURRENT ASSETS	$66,500	TOTAL CURRENT LIABILITIES	$44,500

This showed a potential requirement of $22,000 working capital at December 31st, but she only had $14,500 at June 30th. The same old story: not enough working capital in December. Where could she obtain another $7,500 before December?

One source would be the profits of the business from June to December. The business had been generating a cash gain (net profit plus depreciation) of only $800 per month during the past three years. If this continued from June 30th, 1980, to December 31st, 1980, it would total $4,800, assuming none of it would have to be spent during that period on such things as fixed assets or mortgage payments. Working capital would then increase by this amount, from $14,500 at June 30th to $19,300 by December 31st. But the estimated working capital requirement at December 31st is $22,000. So another $2,700 or so would have to be found.

Debra looked at her balance sheet again. Surely, with her good bank record the local bank would be willing to increase her line of credit. She would offer the bank a $20,000 paid-up personal life insurance policy as security. An increase in bank credit of $2,700 would probably solve her working capital problem for next December. Debra remembered that this was all based on an estimate; so to allow for error and flexibility, she applied for an increase in her line of credit from $7,000 to $12,000. This would give her access to $5,000 more bank credit, if needed. Her application was approved.

She summarized her situation as follows:

Actual working capital at June 30th, 1980	$14,500
Estimated cash gain July 1st — Dec. 31st, 1980	4,800
Estimated working capital Dec. 31st, 1980	19,300
Working capital needed Dec. 31st, 1980	
— using $7,000 line of credit	22,000
— using $12,000 line of credit	17,000

The new line of credit would assure a comfortable working capital position during the coming month of December.

Debra then considered the second type of change in sales volume; the moving up to a new plateau in annual sales. She was planning to open a second store in June, 1981, which should increase her total sales by $100,000 to $340,000 in the first year. So December 1981 would bring another working capital crisis. She expected the second store would just break even the first year so the cash gain during 1981 would continue to be $800 per month. She estimated that the combined balance sheet (current portion) for both stores at December 31st, 1981, would look like this:

Cash	$ 800	Bank advances	$12,000
Receivables	8,500	Accounts payable	53,000
Inventory	85,000		
	$94,300		$65,000

She would need $29,300 working capital, $12,300 more than the $17,000 needed December 31st, 1980, in both cases using the full $12,000 line of credit. Should she try to find some new money herself to invest in the business, or again rely on bank or other credit?

She remembered that the business would gain cash of about 12 × $800 = $9,600 in the twelve months. She decided that she would invest another $5,000 in the business in 1981 to bolster the working capital. She again summarized her thoughts as follows:

Estimated working capital Dec. 31st, 1980	$17,000
(using new $12,000 bank credit)	
Estimated cash gain Jan. 1st — Dec. 31st, 1981	9,600
New investment by owner during 1981	5,000
Estimated working capital available Dec. 31st, 1981	31,600
Working capital required on Dec. 31st, 1981 (estimated)	29,300

Debra was satisfied that this plan would satisfy the working capital needs of the business during the peak period of December, 1981. It provided a small cushion of $2,300 more than the estimated requirement, in case she did not quite meet the estimated figures.

Leduc Cleaners and Drew Drugs are typical small businesses with their own unique requirements for working capital. What is the main reason for the very different working capital needs of each of them? In Bob Leduc's case his inventory requirements are small, about $800 to be paid for within 30 days. Debra Drew, on the other hand, had to have an inventory of $40,000, peaking to $60,000 in December, and she too had to pay her suppliers on 30-day terms. Furthermore, Debra carried $4,000 to $6,000 in accounts receivable, as opposed to Bob's $500. Both businesses have had a successful record, but despite this, serious shortages of working capital could have caused them difficulty, even to the point of failure.

SIGNS OF A POOR WORKING CAPITAL POSITION

How can you detect a poor working capital position? Check the following:

The current ratio (Current assets to current liabilities). There is trouble if it is lower than the industry average.

Acid test ratio (The combined total of cash, accounts receivable, marketable securities to current liabilities). Compare your ratio with the industry average.

Trade payables Look to see if they are increasing. Look also to see if cash discounts are being taken on purchases.

Bank balance Is it sufficient to pay for cheques written on it, or is it plagued by overdrafts?

Loan payments Are they falling behind? Are suppliers insisting on COD's only?

Financial fire fighting Is the owner spending more time looking for financing to eradicate problems rather than directing the business?

CAUSES OF A POOR WORKING CAPITAL POSITION

A poor working capital position can be brought on by one or several of the following causes:

- continuing operational losses
- unusual nonrecurring losses such as theft, fire, lawsuits
- overly generous salaries and raises
- over-investment in fixed assets from working capital
- temporary cash shortage which could be the result of a slow payment of a larger-than-normal receivable
- lax collection policies on accounts receivable

- over-investment in slow-moving inventories
- lack of attention to the business's statements and improper interpretation of the statements

CONCLUSION

The only strict rule of thumb about the amount of working capital a business must maintain is that it be adequate. That means that sufficient cash should be kept on hand to pay for debt obligations as they become due; for payroll disbursements; to benefit from discounts on purchases granted when bills are paid within a specified discount period; to avoid paying penalty fees on unpaid taxes or other such obligations; for the maintenance of a business's good reputation among its suppliers and customers.

6. EQUITY CAPITAL
FOR SMALL COMPANIES

"Most successful small companies reach the point where they are ready to invite partners into the business. This sharing of ownership is a major step requiring careful study and consideration."

— *CASE Counsellor*

INTRODUCTION

As a small business entrepreneur, you will of course want your business to grow in sales, profits, and assets. Growth means expansion. And expansion means additional investment in both fixed and current assets. Ideally, the business's profits should provide the necessary capital for this growth. But too often, instead of using profits, the necessary capital must be sought elsewhere. In most cases, the entrepreneur will approach a term lender. Nevertheless, there is another source: equity financing.

This chapter looks at equity capital for the small company. Beginning with a definition, it examines: why equity capital is needed; what the advantages and disadvantages are; the sources of equity financing. This chapter also includes a section on how to approach an equity investor.

WHY DO YOU NEED EQUITY CAPITAL?

The following situation will best illustrate why a small business entrepreneur may need equity capital.

Henry McCoy and his son Carl, who is the accountant for Henry's business, were shown into the bank manager's office.

Henry McCoy has been in business for six years and his company, 'McCoy Tooling', is doing very well. Because McCoy Tooling is doing so well is the reason that Henry is seeing the bank manager. They are ready to expand operations. New machining equipment and enlarged premises will see a 30% increase in orders.

This is how a portion of the conversation with the bank manager went:

"This is a lot of money that you need," said the bank manager.

"We're not denying it," replied Henry. "My son has all the figures worked out. The sales will justify the money we need."

Carl confirmed the details of the proposal and showed proof of the expected sales.

"We've always paid back our loan on time," pointed out Carl. "Business is very good and these new orders are guaranteed if we have the new equipment and facilities."

"Don't get me wrong," said the bank manager. "You've got an excellent track record and I could lend you the money."

"So do it," interrupted Henry.

"Listen. For this size of loan and for the security aspect, I'm going to have to spread the loan over ten years. Do you realize what the monthly payments will be? All your 30% increase in sales will be used to pay the loan. And if sales take a dip, then you'd be cutting into the level of profits you're now making."

The manager worked out the repayment schedule with Carl and, based on submitted forecasts, the loan became too onerous.

"Does that mean we can't grow?" suddenly demanded Henry.

"Not at all," answered the manager. "What you need is more equity not more debt financing. With an infusion of additional equity you'll be able to expand operations. Getting this money as equity will mean you won't have to pay it back in installments."

"But," said Carl "for us more equity will mean sharing the ownership of the business."

"That," replied the manager, "is part of the definition of equity and part of its advantages and disadvantages."

Equity capital can be required to:
- develop a new idea, product, process, or service - the feasibility of which is as yet unproved
- start a new business that shows a promising future
- develop or expand an existing business
- re-establish an existing business that is potentially profitable but is experiencing financing difficulties
- purchase an existing profitable business

While equity capital can be required for all of the above, it must be understood that certain situations will be more attractive for an equity investment than others. Generally, equity capital is provided without the complete security of assets, so therefore the degree of risk has to be carefully assessed. Proven profitability lessens the degree of risk and increases the attractiveness of an investment.

EQUITY CAPITAL DEFINED

Simply stated, **equity capital is that part of the money invested in the business which is not debt**. Stated another way, money is invested into the business which does not have to be repaid in specified installments. Equity capital as an investment is a long-term commitment. However, while it does not have to be paid back in the short term, in the long term it may be paid back if the business is sold, if a partner or partners are bought out, or if shares change hands.

As we have stated previously, equity capital as an investment has a higher risk than does debt financing. Debt financing is usually secured by the business's assets. This is not always so with equity financing. Because of this, the equity investor is looking for a return on the investment by sharing as an owner in the business's profits.

Equity capital, therefore, is termed ownership dollars. This ownership is divided into three categories:

> sole ownership
> partnership
> limited company

Let us look at each category from the point of view of equity capital.

Sole ownership   The equity capital in your business is derived from your personal savings, securities, real estate, and money borrowed from family and friends. Your equity capital may also be a result of a term loan secured by your personal assets such as your house. As a sole owner, you are responsible for your business's assets and liabilities. As well, the profit or loss of the business is yours alone.

Partnership   If you don't have enough money from your own sources (described under sole ownership) and you can't or do not wish to go to a lender, you can obtain equity capital through the addition of one or more partners. A partner or partners provide you with the money you need, but they then become part owners of the business and, as such, share in the profits as well as the losses.

You will have to determine with your partner or partners how much of the business you are going to share. This depends on the amount of money invested as equity capital as well as their share in management decisions. They may be silent partners, where all they do is provide the money and you provide the expertise, or they may be working partners, where they share both money and know-how.

Partners can be either general or limited. General partners are working and active in the business and are liable for any debts or obligations of the business. Limited partners only contribute money and cannot be held liable for the business's debts or obligations.

Limited Company The third way of obtaining capital is to become a limited company. A limited company means that you have incorporated your business and can sell shares of the business to a number of specified people. Your business becomes a separate entity from yourself and others who own it. You are all shareholders.

The majority of small businesses which incorporate are private companies. This means that, legally, there is a restriction on the number of shareholders as well as the transfer of shares. The value of the shares and the amount are determined at the time of sale. Control over the business is dictated by who has the greatest amount of shares. Should the business fail, each shareholder is only liable for the shares that he or she has purchased but not yet paid for.

ADVANTAGES AND DISADVANTAGES OF USING EQUITY CAPITAL

When you have obtained equity capital from sources other than your own, you will no longer be in the category of sole ownership. You will be sharing the ownership of your business. Before taking this step, it is wise to look at the advantages and disadvantages of outside equity capital.

The advantages are:

- it permits faster growth of the business because of readily available money
- it allows expansion of the business's borrowing power in case additional debt financing is needed
- the business may acquire a better reputation and credibility than it could obtain on its own. As well, the business's credit rating with its suppliers can be improved
- outside equity monies normally do not have to be repaid (on a regular basis) and, therefore, they don't drain the business's cash flow
- outside equity capital brings with it not only money, but the investors' advice and expertise in many aspects of management
- because the outside investors have a vested interest in the business, they usually can be approached for continuing support of the business
- by spreading the business's ownership over more partners or shareholders, the business may be more venturesome than if there was only one owner

The disadvantages are:

- loss of flexibility. You will have to share control of the business and will not be the only boss anymore
- sharing ownership means you have a reduced share in the business's profits
- there may be additional expenses such as administrative, accounting, and legal fees. For example, there will be legal costs for drawing up a partnership agreement or for incorporating, and accounting and administrative costs for issuing dividends and keeping records

WHERE DO YOU OBTAIN EQUITY CAPITAL?

As we saw in one of our previous sections, equity capital was defined by three categories: sole ownership, partnership, and limited company. Sole ownership means your own sources of capital. Partnership and limited company mean an outside equity investor. Where do you find the outside equity investor?

The outside equity sources available to the small business can be divided into private and non-private.

Private sources Includes friends and relatives who may be willing to take a share of the ownership in turn for investing their money. Employees may be another source. If incorporated, shares could be sold to employees as a form of employee profit-sharing. Customers and suppliers may also be interested in investing in your business. However, these last two sources could result in undue restrictions on your business's operations and could make other customers and suppliers reluctant to deal with you.

Often your bank manager, accounting firm, or lawyer will be able to direct you to one of their other clients who may be interested in taking an equity position in a promising, small business.

Non-private sources Mainly venture capital firms. These are often owned by a consortium of banks, trust companies, or other pools of capital. They specialize in investing in businesses that have a strong growth potential and offer a good realization on investment.

Another non-private source available to a small business is the larger company usually operating in the same field. The motive for a larger company to invest in a smaller one can vary. It can be to control a smaller competitor, to buy an interest in a development process that the larger company may one day value, or to retain contact with an individual whose business may eventually be of use to the larger concern.

HOW THE OUTSIDE INVESTOR
LOOKS AT A BUSINESS

Because the equity investor is making a long-term commitment to a business, he or she will want to be sure that certain factors are present in order for the investment to be realized. Let us examine some of the major factors an equity investor considers when approached by a business for equity capital.

Potential for growth   The equity investor is looking for significant growth potential in a business that will warrant the infusion of money. Often the value of the original investment in a business is expected to appreciate significantly in the first three years.

Management   The equity investor will be very interested in evaluating the competency of the business's management, whether it consists of just the owner or a management team. The quality of competency often conditions the degree of the risk of failure and the potential for growth.

The amount of equity   The equity investor will assess the amount of money to be invested in the business in relation to how long it will take for the majority or all of the investment to be realized.

Controls   Equity investors, either as partners or major shareholders, will always want to protect their investment. The investor's degree of involvement in the daily operations of the business will depend on the arrangements made with the original owner. Regardless of the day-to-day involvement, most equity investors will wish to provide input concerning large capital expenditures, long-term commitments, and any other major events that could affect the overall financial structure of the business.

Selling the investment   While equity capital is a long-term commitment, the investor will want to have a good idea at what point he or she could sell the investment. The equity capital position could be sold to: other partners, other private shareholders, an outsider or, if the business is large enough, the public on the stock market. Once the funds are released, the investor is then free to reinvest the money elsewhere.

Equity investors will do all they can to protect their interests. As well, investors will take all the necessary precautions before committing funds. A business, therefore, must look very attractive as an investment.

To help make your proposal for equity capital attractive, the following section will show how to approach an equity investor.

HOW TO APPROACH THE EQUITY INVESTOR

You can't expect an outside investor to commit money for something that is not planned. Whatever your reasons for seeking equity capital, you must present your case to the investor in a convincing and professional way. It is essential that you document the investment proposal. In short, you must present an equity investor with a well thought-out and realistic business proposal.

Your business proposal should be a very detailed document that answers five crucial questions:

- Is there competent management and is it sufficient for all aspects of the business's operations?
- Does the business have an edge in market, market strategy, product, and service?
- Are the assets of high value and are the business's facilities adequate for the product and service?
- Is there sufficient funding to ensure long-term continuity?
- How will the business grow?

It is to your advantage to present the equity investor with as much information as possible. Your proposal must be professional in appearance and it must be supported by realistic documentation. Be prepared to sell your business yet don't exaggerate as the equity investor will be sharing the ownership of your business and will become aware of any misrepresentation.

The information to appear in your proposal may include:

- a resume of the business
- a resume of the principals and key people
- a description of labour (wage earners and staff)

- marketing details
- research and development details
- operational details
- past financial statements
- future profit and loss statements
- cash flow statements
- personal financial statements
- list of security available
- goals and objectives of the business
- leases, patents, insurance policies, union agreements, mortgage copies, liens, and similar

Remember, above all, that your proposal must show how the new equity capital is going to be used and why. To appeal to an equity investor, your proposal must have strong evidence of growth potential and demonstrate that it is a good investment. When preparing such a proposal, you may wish to consider the services of a professional accountant.

CONCLUSION

The owner of a small business seeking additional equity capital from outside sources should keep three key points in mind:

- plan carefully, thoroughly, and for the long term
- demonstrate to potential investors that management is competent and that growth prospects are good
- convince prospective investors that the offer of an ownership interest is on terms at least as attractive as other investment opportunities open to them

Outside equity capital means sharing the ownership of your business. So when approaching an outside equity investor for funds, remember you will be sharing the ownership of your business with this person or persons for many years. Choose the equity investor carefully and, ideally, get one who brings to your business more than just money.

7. MANAGING YOUR CURRENT ASSETS

"Good management, or the lack of it, has a major effect on the condition of your current assets."

— CASE Counsellor

INTRODUCTION

Current assets are what a business owns in the way of cash or things that can be converted to cash within one year. Therefore, aside from actual cash, current assets include: quickly marketable securities such as bonds, inventories that can be sold for cash or on credit, and accounts receivable which represent cash paid in installments.

Managing your current assets means more than managing the amount of each of these components: cash, inventory, and accounts receivable. It means managing the flow of cash as it is converted to inventory, then to accounts receivable, then back to cash.

The cash cycle in a business i.e. from cash to inventory to accounts receivable to cash, is like the cycle in nature when water in a lake evaporates to form clouds, which in turn form droplets which fall as rain into the lake. Just as a drought may occur if a lake evaporates but condensation in the form of raindrops does not refill it, so too can a business's cash resources dry up, preventing the acquisition of new inventory, the sales of which would replenish the cash resources.

The owner of a business must ensure that this flow is not interrupted by having cash tied up almost exclusively in slow-moving inventory or in aging accounts receivable.

This chapter will focus on the current assets of 'Small Enterprises Ltd.' and will illustrate ways to effectively manage cash resources, accounts receivable, and inventories. The methods shown can be used for a comparable business.

LISTING YOUR CURRENT ASSETS

As the owner of a small business, how much of your investment should be in current, as opposed to fixed, assets?

To ascertain this proportion, you must find out how much cash, accounts receivable, and inventories your business needs. These needs occur when you start-up, when you are operating during busy and quiet seasons, and when you wish to expand.

Let us take a look at the balance sheet of Small Enterprises Ltd.

Small Enterprises Ltd.
Balance Sheet — December 31st, 1980

ASSETS		LIABILITIES	
Cash on hand	$ 200	Bank Loan	$4,000
Cash in bank	2,000	Accounts payable	2,000
Canada Savings Bonds	1,000		
Accounts receivable	5,500		
Inventories	7,000		
Total Current Assets	$15,700	Total Current Liabilities	$6,000

Note that its assets are listed in order of ease of convertibility to cash, starting with cash itself.

Let us suppose that this business is selling about $5,000 in goods or services per month during the winter. Is it managing its current assets effectively?

CASH

Most small businesses need a petty cash fund to take care of daily expenses. The question is: how much cash? And the answer is: as much as the business needs to meet its cash requirements on a day-to-day basis.

To find out how much the business needs, owners should prepare cash flow forecasts (described in detail in the chapter entitled "Managing your Cash") which show on a month-to-month basis what cash they estimate they will receive, what cash they will have to pay out, and where they will have cash surpluses or shortages.

From such a forecast, they will know how much cash they should keep on hand on a day-to-day basis.

Is the $200 that Small Enterprises Ltd. keeps on hand sufficient? For day-to-day operations, yes. The amount should be kept to a minimum — just enough to take care of the business's needs — because cash on hand does not generate a return on investment.

The $2,000 cash in bank, on the other hand, looks excessive for normal operations of the business. The company is receiving bank credit, and unless this relatively large deposit was needed for a special purpose at the balance sheet date, it seems unjustified. Likewise, the investment in Canada Savings Bonds might be better employed in financing the operation of the business.

With reference to the need to manage the flow of cash through the business, Small Enterprises Ltd. is not putting its cash into the flow. Too much of its cash resources is static. The business's growth may be stunted.

ACCOUNTS RECEIVABLE

The chapter, "Giving Credit to your Customers", outlines briefly some of the principles of a credit system for a small business. The amount of your accounts receivable, the amount owed to your business by customers for goods or services you sold them on credit, will depend to a large extent on the rules you have set up for granting credit to your customers and the way you apply them. If your credit terms are vague and your invoicing system sluggish, your accounts receivable will tie up too much of your investment. This costs your business money.

There are two simple ways of keeping an eye on your accounts receivable.

1. Aging your receivables

One is to age them, that is to classify them according to their age since the date of sale. In the case of Small Enterprises Ltd., an aging of the $5,500 accounts receivable at December 31st, 1980, shows the following:

Receivables outstanding less than 30 days	$4,400	80%
Receivables outstanding 30 to 60 days	770	14%
Receivables outstanding over 60 days	330	6%
	$5,500	100%

If the selling terms of this business are net 30 days, 20 percent of its receivables are overdue. If these overdue accounts didn't exist, the $1,100 tied up in them could be put to use in producing more goods or services for sale.

The aging analysis, made up from a listing of all your individual accounts receivable, can be done quite quickly on a regular basis, for example, at the end of each week or month. If you know your customers, you will also know from the aging analysis what quality the overdue accounts have, that is, what likelihood there is of collecting each, or whether a bad debt loss might be expected from some.

You can also see from examining the accounts receivable whether any overdue amounts comprise mainly one or two large accounts. Just ask your bookkeeper to list separately the accounts overdue in amounts of more than, say, $100 or an appropriate amount that is large for your business. In the preceding example, it might be that the $330 outstanding over 60 days is all due from one customer. If steps to collect from this one customer were applied successfully, the accounts receivable picture would improve sharply.

You can also determine, from the aging schedules for several consecutive periods, whether your collections are improving or whether old accounts are piling up. This might suggest a need for changing your credit terms and collection practices.

2. Calculating your average collection period

If your credit and collection system is under control, the level of your accounts receivable will likely vary directly with sales volume. Another simple test is to calculate the average collection period. The formula for calculating your annual average collection period is:

$$\text{Average Collection Period} = \frac{\text{Accounts Receivable}}{\text{Annual Sales}} \times 365 \text{ days}$$

If Small Enterprises Ltd. had sales of $75,000 in 1980, the accounts receivable of $5,500 at the end of that year represent about 27 days' sales ($5,500 ÷ $75,000 × 365 days). The average collection period is, therefore, 27 days. It would be even more accurate to calculate the average collection period by using the average of the accounts receivable at the beginning and at the end of the year. Also, the calculation could be based on business days in the year, rather than calendar days. This involves a bit more work, but the main point is to do it the same way each time.

The average collection period can also be calculated on a monthly basis, each month-end. If December 1980 was a slow month for Small Enterprises Ltd., with sales of only $5,000, the accounts receivable of $5,500 at the month-end were 34 days' sales ($5,500 × $5,000 × 31). This is higher than the year's average collection period of 27 days' sales, and might be an indication of a slow-down in collections. If so, steps should be taken to urge more prompt payment by customers. On the other hand, it could be that the business normally gives more credit in December than at other times of the year. The circumstances will indicate what collection steps, if any, are required and care should be taken to achieve the best results with a minimum of offence to customers.

INVENTORIES

To control your investment in inventories you need to know regularly what quantities of materials, supplies, and finished goods your business requires in stock and what value to give to them.

The inventory of a manufacturing business will normally include raw materials, goods in process, finished goods, parts, and supplies, such as the packaging materials for the finished products. In non-manufacturing businesses the inventory may consist of supplies or finished goods, or both.

Consider first the size of inventory required. It is common practice in many businesses to take a physical count of the entire inventory at the end of each business month. This tells you how much inventory you actually have. But how much should you have for good control of your investment?

Generally speaking, the smaller the inventory you can carry and still not run into shortages and slow deliveries to customers, the better. So you should know how fast your finished goods inventory moves out of your business to your customers, that is, how fast it turns over. Unfortunately, most businesses cannot stock their products just to meet firm orders. They have to have additional goods on hand at all times. Your customers expect you to supply exactly what they want when they need it, or they will buy elsewhere. A complete inventory is needed, including fast-moving and some slow-moving items, but your business should not be overburdened with the latter. If you know where you can get some of these items quickly, perhaps in one day's delivery, you may not need to stock them. You should also know what minimum and maximum inventories you need for your slow and busy sales seasons.

Small Enterprises Ltd. is a manufacturer, and $2,800 of its year-end inventory of $7,000 was raw materials. This amounted to about 17 days' sales, with December sales of $5,000. January sales were expected to be the same. The company had found from experience that 17 days' sales was an adequate inventory of raw materials to keep its production running on schedule. Alternatively, the company could compare its inventory with its purchases rather than sales, and express the inventory as so many days' purchases. It forecast its sales and corresponding material purchases for each month of the coming year using the formula:

$$\text{Avg. Raw Material Inventory} = \frac{17 \text{ (days' sales)}}{31 \text{ (days in mo.)}} \times \text{ Monthly Sales}$$

The company then bought its raw materials in advance accordingly. For a month in which $8,000 sales were forecast, it would increase its raw materials level to about $4,500, 17 days' sales. This requires a close watch on purchasing and familiarity with delivery times, price changes, and discounts available.

Small Enterprises Ltd. had a goods-in-process inventory valued at $200 at December 31st. This was the value of the partly-finished products in the plant at the end of that day. In some circumstances this can be reduced by speeding up the plant either mechanically or by using more labour, or by improving the scheduling of production.

This company had finished goods worth $4,000 at December 31st. There were ten different products and each item was recorded on a card showing the quantity on hand, its value, and the re-order point. When the quantity was reduced to this re-order amount, the company would produce or re-order that product. Inventory control systems are described in many readily-available publications.

In many businesses, such as this one, a small percentage of the inventory items account for a large percentage of sales. Small Enterprises Ltd. found its breakdown to be:

Products	% of Inventory	% of Sales
1 and 2	20	75
3, 4 and 5	30	15
6 to 10 inclusive	50	10

Obviously, products 1 and 2, the fast movers, should receive close attention in the inventory as they account for 75 percent of the company's sales. The finished goods inventory can be reduced if more firm orders are obtained, and production is scheduled for their immediate delivery.

Another way of determining whether your inventory is too large or too small for the size of your business is to compare it by each category with your average monthly sales for the preceding several months. Six months is a suggested period of time.

Small Enterprises Ltd. had the following sales for the last half of 1980:

Month	Sales
July	$ 8,000
August	8,000
September	7,000
October	6,000
November	5,000
December	5,000
6 Months Total Sales	$39,000
Average Monthly Sales	$ 6,500

The total inventory of $7,000 at December 31st was, therefore, about 32 days' average sales. The company had found that a total inventory of about 30 days' average sales was sufficient for normal operations and had gradually reduced it for the fall and winter, its slack season. It would continue to reduce it to about $6,500.

So much for the quantities of inventory required by a business. How do you price the quantities?

A simple method is to price each item at cost or market value, whichever is lower. This avoids overstating the value of your inventory in the event of a decline in the selling price of certain items.

In pricing the finished goods inventory in some businesses, certain items may also lose all or part of their value because of spoilage, a sharp change in fashions, or other factors.

EXPANDING YOUR BUSINESS

If the sales of your business are increasing sharply, or if you plan an expansion to increase your sales, you should also plan what current assets your business will have at the new sales volume. Generally speaking, your accounts receivable and inventories will increase, but normally you would not need more cash on hand or on deposit.

Small Enterprises Ltd. had sales of $75,000 in 1980, 20 percent more than its volume of $62,500 the year before. It had studied its orders and markets carefully and forecast sales of $90,000 in 1981, another 20 percent increase. This would be more than the plant could produce unless it added another machine early in 1981. The company decided to buy the machine and it would be in production in March. What investment would it need in current assets at this higher level of sales?

Cash on hand of $200 could be maintained but the $2,000 cash in bank and $1,000 Canada Savings Bond could be spent on new materials and supplies. Accounts receivable would be expected to increase to $6,650, still averaging 27 days' sales at the new sales volume, i.e.: 27 ÷ 365 × $90,000.

Based on the past, the average raw material inventory should be increased to about $4,200, or 17 days' sales (17 ÷ 365 × $90,000). Its goods-in-process would likely increase due to the additional machine to perhaps $240. Similarly, 20 percent more finished goods, i.e., $4,800 on the average, might be needed to fill the additional orders, although this would depend on the new higher production rate and the proportions of items being sold. This would mean a total inventory of $9,240, rather than the former level of $7,000.

In summary, the old and new levels of inventory would be as follows:

	1980 Sales $75,000	1981 Sales $90,000
Raw materials	$ 2,800	$ 4,200
Goods in process	200	240
Finished goods	4,000	4,800
Total Inventory	$ 7,000	$ 9,240

The current part of the company's balance sheet might look like this during the next peak sales period, say June 30th, 1981.

Small Enterprises Ltd.
Balance Sheet — June 30, 1981

ASSETS		LIABILITIES	
Cash on hand	$ 200	Bank Loan	$3,000
Accounts receivable	6,650	Accounts payable	2,400
Inventories	9,240		
Total Current Assets	$16,090	Total Current Liabilities	$5,400

CONCLUSION

Aging of receivables, calculating the collection period, and analyzing the inventory by size and products are a few simple checks that can guide you in managing your current assets. If done regularly, they can help you to keep your investment in current assets at a level your business needs so as to function day-by-day, and to grow year-by-year.

8. MANAGING YOUR FIXED ASSETS

"Fixed assets don't produce sales, but they should produce profits."
— CASE Counsellor

INTRODUCTION

Fixed assets are the assets a business requires to enable it to make sales and, if necessary, to produce the goods and services it has for sale.

Fixed assets differ from current assets in two respects:

• they are not for sale (unless disposed of under special circumstances such as relocation)
• they remain in the business for longer than a year

Fixed assets include: land, buildings, machinery, equipment, vehicles, furniture, fixtures, and patents. They do not get used up or consumed in the same way as the materials used to manufacture products or services for sale. However, a part of the useful life of fixed assets goes into the production of each of the business's products and services. Fixed assets can be expected to lose value as they deteriorate or break down during their lifetime. Only land does not depreciate, although in special cases, such as land containing mineral reserves, the value may depreciate with the depletion of the natural resource.

This chapter will focus on the major ways of managing your fixed assets. The purpose of managing fixed assets is to keep fixed expenses such as interest and depreciation under control so that you can keep your selling prices competitive.

THE VALUE AND DEPRECIATION OF YOUR FIXED ASSETS

Like current assets, fixed assets are listed on the left side of your balance sheet. They appear below the current assets, and are listed in the order of their expected useful life. Assets with the longest expected life are listed first as in the following example:

Land	$ 2,000
Buildings	20,000
Furniture and fixtures	2,000
Machinery and equipment	10,000
Vehicles	3,500

The value shown initially on the balance sheet for each type of fixed asset is normally the cost incurred by the business to acquire the assets. Obviously, equipment, buildings, and vehicles deteriorate with use. Their value decreases so that they are no longer worth their original price. Each year, therefore, their book value is reduced to reflect that deterioration. The amount of that reduction is charged as an expense to the business for the year, and is shown on the profit and loss statement for the year as a depreciation expense or depletion allowance.

There are various optional methods to calculate depreciation of fixed assets, among them: the straight-line method; the payback method; the rate of return method; and, the net present value method. When choosing one of them, take into consideration your business's size and profit picture. Seek the advice of an accountant. Have this person explain the particular benefits of each method and recommend the one best suited to your business.

Not optional, but mandatory, is the diminishing balance method which you must use when calculating the income tax payable by your business. According to this method, you reduce the book value of each fixed asset by a fixed percentage each year. The federal Income Tax Act stipulates what maximum percentage of book value you can charge as a tax-exempt business expense for each type of fixed asset. By this method, the amount of depreciation charged keeps reducing year by year as the book value reduces each year.

One of the simplest methods and the one most commonly used by businesses for their own records is the straight-line method. According to this method, a fixed asset is depreciated by the same amount for each year of its useful life. Thus, if a new machine costing $1,000 is expected to be used for ten years, and to have a salvage value of zero after that time, $100 of depreciation would be charged in each of the ten years that the machine is used.

On the balance sheet, these yearly charges for depreciation are accumulated as follows:

		Book Value after Accumulated Depreciation
Land		$ 2,000
Buildings	$20,000	
Less Accumulated Depreciation	2,000	18,000
Furniture and fixtures	2,000	
Less Accumulated Depreciation	200	1,800
Machinery and equipment	10,000	
Less Accumulated Depreciation	2,000	8,000
Vehicles	3,500	
Less Accumulated Depreciation	1,050	2,450

Let us now look at each of the major assets that can constitute the term fixed assets.

LAND

The initial price of the land is only one consideration when you are looking for a site for your business. Location is another. Where is your market? Where do you get your materials and labour? Is the shape of the site suitable for your building and operation? Is there good access to it? Is it completely serviced? What are the taxes? Are there any zoning or other restrictions about building? Is parking space adequate? Such considerations may be more important to the long-term success of your business than the initial price of land.

No matter what site you select, don't forget about future expansion. If the sales of your business increase 10 percent per year, they will double about every seven and a half years. If they increase 15 percent per year, they will double every five years. This kind of sales growth requires more space and the regular addition of other facilities. Is your land site large enough for such growth, or alternatively, would it be feasible to move the business to a larger site in five or ten years? A site that is too large for your present requirements need not remain idle. Lease the excess space to another business until you require it for your own expansion. Rental income from that portion of your land can then be available for working capital.

BUILDINGS

Before selecting a building for your business, you should give careful thought to the arrangement of the machinery, equipment, and work areas inside the building. Prepare a layout of the floor area on paper, using moveable blocks of heavy paper representing to scale every major piece of equipment, machinery, etc.

Picture in your mind how the people and materials will move in your building. Then move the models around on paper to give you the most efficient arrangement. This should result in a smooth flow of traffic without too much criss-crossing. It should also provide easy passage of goods into the receiving area and out of the shipping area. If you don't feel qualified to make your own plant layout, hire a consulting engineer to do it for you. But above all, do prepare a layout! Moving a machine on paper ahead of time is much cheaper than moving the actual machine from a bad location later. Why not visit a few buildings used for the same type of business? Study their layouts, and you may benefit from their experience, or from their oversights.

Don't forget about future expansion, either horizontal, or vertical, or both. If you expect to expand horizontally, your plans might call for a temporary wall on one side, adjoining the vacant land area on which you will expand. If you are thinking of vertical expansion, make sure the building columns are designed to support a second storey.

Common-purpose buildings are the most readily saleable, so avoid, if possible, any special features that would detract from the building's attraction to other businesses. You might want to sell it or rent it sometime. A standard pre-fabricated building, adaptable to most purposes, might have more appeal to a prospective tenant than a custom-designed building.

Heat, water, electric power, and waste disposal are services your building will require. You will need to know what type and quantity of each of these services will be needed before deciding on the equipment and distribution for your building. You may have to install pollution controls for your type of business. You may also need air-conditioning, refrigeration, and special materials-handling equipment such as power conveyors. Suppliers of this equipment can help you select the best size for your purpose.

Choosing a suitable, fully-serviced building is one of the most important business decisions you will have to make. When you have taken stock of all of your requirements, get professional help for the final design, for the obtaining of a construction contract by tender, and for the supervision of construction.

As previously mentioned, the federal Income Tax Act allows you to charge each year, as a business expense which will not be taxed, an amount for the depreciation of your building, if it is owned by your business. Assume current maximum depreciation rates are 10 percent per year on frame buildings and 5 percent per year on brick or masonry buildings. Apply these percentages to the book value of the building, that is, the cost less the depreciation you have charged to date on the building, using the diminishing balance method.

Suppose you are considering the purchase of a warehouse building. Two new buildings of the same size are available, one of steel frame and brick construction, and the other of wood frame and siding. Which should you buy? There are several methods of comparing, in financial terms, the relative merits of alternative choices of fixed assets, such as buildings. The total annual cost method is one you could use. A comparison could take the following form:

DATA	Building A Steel & Brick	Building B Wood
Initial cost	$120,000	$56,000
Interest rate	15%	15%
Depreciation	5%	10%
Taxes	8%	8%
Fire insurance, annual, per $100		
Building	2.00	5.00
Contents (Value $30,000)	2.50	6.00
Business loss insurance	1,200	1,400
Operating cost disadvantage	—	1,000
ANNUAL COST		
Interest	18,000	8,400
Depreciation	6,000	5,600
Taxes	9,600	4,480
Fire insurance, building	2,400	2,800
contents	750	1,800
Business loss insurance	1,200	1,400
Operating cost disadvantage	—	1,000
TOTAL ANNUAL COST	$ 37,950	$25,480

In this case, the wooden building should be purchased because of its lower annual cost.

FURNITURE AND FIXTURES

You need comfortable, quiet offices where you and your employees will function effectively, and where you can conduct your business in an organized manner.

In some businesses, it makes good business sense to decorate your office interiors to create a fashionable image, and to display the goods, workmanship, and services of your business in an appealing way. In such cases, some extra investment in furniture and fixtures is warranted. But don't overlook the fact that good service is usually a far more compelling force in attracting and keeping customers than luxurious, expensive office furniture.

MACHINERY AND EQUIPMENT

James Watt, who patented one of the first practical steam engines in 1769, said: "Of all things, but proverbially so in mechanics, the supreme excellence is simplicity." This is particularly true of machinery and equipment for a small business, where high initial costs and subsequent maintenance costs for overly sophisticated models may be prohibitive. In fact, such machines may cause excessive stoppages of production, where a simpler model would keep running.

When selecting equipment you need to be specific about what it should do for you. How many units of your product should the machine handle in a given time to meet your sales requirements? How many operators can you afford to run it? How much space is available for it? What quality must it be able to produce? There's probably a machine available to meet your basic requirements. So make the machine match your requirements. If you were to purchase a sophisticated machine on impulse, and then try to make your plant match the requirements of the machine, you would be wasting some of the money you have invested in your business.

If you are manufacturing products, it is your machinery, equipment, and employees that will make profits for your business — not land, buildings, and furniture. Search for simple, good quality machinery and equipment at the lowest cost rather than top-of-the-line items at high cost.

Suppose you are considering the purchase of a machine for your business such as a power lathe for your machine shop. A common method for analyzing such a purchase is the payback method. Will the savings from the machine pay for the machine before it wears out? A lathe might be available for $4,000 that would last you 8 years and would save you $1,000 in labour each year. The payback period would be:

$$\frac{\$4,000}{\$1,000} = 4 \text{ years.}$$

This sounds attractive because the lathe would pay for itself in much less than its expected useful life. You should probably buy it. But is there a better buy available?

Another supplier will sell you a more versatile lathe for $6,000 that should last 10 years and should save you $1,500 in labour each year. The payback period would be:

$$\frac{\$6,000}{\$1,500} = 4 \text{ years.}$$

the same as the first example, so this one sounds attractive, too. Now what do you do to choose between them? Look at the expected useful life of each machine. The $4,000 lathe will pay for itself in 4 years, or 50 percent of its useful life of 8 years. But the $6,000 lathe will pay for itself in 4 years, only 40 percent of its useful life of 10 years. Your best investment is the $6,000 machine, which pays for itself relatively sooner in its useful life.

Consider leasing as an alternative to purchasing machinery or equipment. The following factors favour it:

Potential obsolescence If the machinery or equipment required for your business were to become obsolete in a short time, leasing is preferable to purchasing. This factor is especially important when the acquisition of computer hardware is contemplated.

Imminent government regulations If government regulations, especially in the areas of permissible energy consumption levels or pollution control levels, were to require expensive modifications to your equipment, lease the equipment until the regulations become effective.

Need for working capital Leasing frees cash for this purpose.

VEHICLES

Does your business need to own vehicles at all? If the answer is yes, consider leasing vehicles, particularly if you require one or two new ones all the time for sales purposes. On the other hand, if you need a light delivery truck, you would probably use it for several years and then sell it for scrap or trade it in. Purchasing, rather than leasing, such a vehicle would probably be wise because the average annual cost over its lifetime would be quite low.

The factors favouring the leasing of machinery and equipment also apply to vehicles. There are two kinds of leases to choose when leasing a truck: the capital lease and the operating lease. The capital lease is generally long-term. The accumulated payments nearly equal the truck's purchase price. The advantage of such a lease is that a business can use the capital lease as a substitute for a loan to purchase. If a fleet is being leased, the interest charges may be well below the prime rate. A disadvantage is that the lessee must be willing to maintain, operate, and dispose of the trucks involved.

With an operating lease, the lessee pays only for the use of the truck when he or she needs it. The lessor provides the maintenance and insurance and disposes of the truck when the lease expires. However, the truck is not counted on the lessee's books as an asset, although this may be negotiable. Operating leases are generally more expensive than capital leases because of the services provided.

Owning vehicles involves a business in two kinds of expenses: fixed expenses and variable expenses. The fixed expenses for a vehicle are those you will have to pay regardless of how much you use the vehicle, even if it remains in your parking lot most of the time. These fixed expenses include insurance, license fees, seasonal servicing, and, of course, depreciation. Generally speaking, the more expensive vehicles have the higher fixed expenses. Variable expenses are those which will vary according to the number of miles a vehicle is driven. Variable expenses for a vehicle mean the cost of fuel, oil, tires, spark plugs, and other replacement parts. As a rule of thumb, the further a vehicle is driven, the lower the average variable expenses per mile. And a more expensive vehicle does not necessarily have much higher variable expenses than a cheaper one.

The following situation will illustrate what must be considered when purchasing a vehicle:

The decision whether to buy an $8,000 car or a $12,000 car plagued Karen Bancroft for weeks. Her interior decorating business, though still in its infancy, was growing steadily. Given the size of the business, the $8,000 car seemed appropriate. But because so much of her time was spent escorting clients to warehouse showrooms to look at wallpaper designs and carpet samples, she wanted a car that would be comfortable for herself and her clients. The car was also to serve as a kind of mobile office in which she would talk shop with her clients.

To help her decide which car to choose, she compared the major fixed and variable expenses expected for each car. She assumed that whichever car was bought would be replaced in three years with a certain trade-in value. Before totalling her fixed expenses, she made the following assumptions:

	Car A Price $8,000	Car B Price $12,000
Replacement period	3 years	3 years
Trade-in value in 3 years (estimate)	$4,000	$6,000
Cash outlay at replacement	$4,000	$6,000

When listing her fixed expenses such as insurance, license, seasonal tune-ups, 20 car washes per year at $5 per wash, she included $1,333 per year for Car A's replacement (1/3 of cash outlay at replacement), and $2,000 per year for Car B. She discovered that total fixed expenses for Car A would be about $3,000, and for Car B, almost $4,000.

Among the variable expenses, Karen included the cost of: fuel (cents per kilometre); tire replacement every 35,000 kilometres; replacement of oil, oil filters, spark plugs, shock absorbers, winter tires, etc. Total variable expenses for Car A came to $0.098 per kilometre, and for Car B, $0.111 per kilometre.

Karen's figures showed her that the operating cost for both cars at low mileage is high and well above leasing rates for similar cars. But at

30,000 or 40,000 kilometres per year, the higher-priced model became relatively more attractive i.e. the cost per kilometre was not much higher than the cheaper model. Also, at the same higher mileages, leasing rates were less attractive in comparison. Karen now had all the evidence she needed to purchase Car B.

INTANGIBLE ASSETS

The fixed assets, described to this point, are tangible fixed assets. In other words, they have physical substance. Fixed assets can also be intangible, for example, things used in the operation of the business which do not have physical properties, such as patents or copyrights. The value of such intangible assets is in the rights which their possession gives to your business. Even intangible assets have a limited useful life and their value, or cost, in most cases, may be charged off gradually as a business expense during their estimated useful life. The systematic write-off for intangible assets is usually called amortization. It is a similar idea to depreciation for tangible fixed assets (except natural resource fixed assets, such as mineral or timber rights, for which the term depletion is used).

Some intangible fixed assets may have an indefinite useful life. Examples are: goodwill, rights, and franchises without a termination date. These may also be amortized; otherwise, they might have the effect of overstating your balance sheet at a later date. Such assets as goodwill have been known to become valueless during the life of a business.

CONCLUSION

The fixed assets of your business, though not sold like products or services, have a direct bearing on your selling prices. A part of their original value goes into the production of your goods or services during their useful life, except in the case of land.

This wearing out of fixed assets, or depreciation, is a business expense. It is an allowable deduction from the income of your business before taxation.

Before choosing fixed assets, you should consider not only their cost, but the future expansion needs of your business. Alternatives, such as leasing certain fixed assets, or purchasing used items should also be considered. Whether leased or purchased, your fixed assets should contribute to your business's profits.

Good management of your fixed assets will keep your fixed expenses, such as interest and depreciation, under control and your selling prices competitive.

9. MANAGING YOUR CASH

"It is not uncommon for businesses to make profits and yet be in trouble because they don't have ready cash to pay current bills."
— CASE Counsellor

INTRODUCTION

Almost every decision the small business entrepreneur must make has financial implications. Being a good financial manager is, therefore, crucial to the business's success.

One important aspect of financial management is handling the business's cash. You need readily available money to run your business on a day-to-day basis. Inevitably there are suppliers presenting you with bills, some of which may be higher than anticipated. A sudden repair to your premises may be more than expected. You must account for expenses such as these.

Lack of sufficient cash may result in serious problems. Too much cash, however, is a waste of the business's resources. A balance between the two extremes can be achieved with good cash management. The most important tool of cash management is the cash flow forecast, which will help you determine how much cash you need and when.

This chapter will acquaint you with the basic principles of cash management. It will discuss the need for, and the purpose of cash management and will illustrate the preparation of a cash flow forecast.

WHY MANAGE YOUR CASH?

Unfortunately, many small businesses learn too late the answer to the question: Why manage your cash? The following situation is a good illustration of why cash management is so important to the success of a small business:

Cathy and Madeline are partners in a new toy shop in the town's mall. They have been in business now for over a year and are showing a good profit. Yet paying bills always seems to be a problem for them.

"Cathy, the man is here with the teddy bear shipment."

"Tell him to put it in the back."

"Where to put it isn't the problem," explained Madeline. "It's been sent COD because we missed our payment last month."

"Darn it. We need those bears. And I can't write a cheque. How much is the bill?"

"It's almost $450," answered Madeline. "Is there enough in the cash register?"

"I'm not sure," said Cathy opening the till. "I hate taking money out like this when I haven't balanced the till and tape for the last couple of days."

"Let me see how much is in the petty cash box," offered Madeline. "I took some money out yesterday. I forgot to put in a voucher, but I think there's almost a hundred dollars."

By combining the money in the cash register with the hundred dollars from petty cash, Cathy and Madeline were able to pay the COD shipment.

"I don't understand," said Madeline later that afternoon as they were placing the teddies on the shelves. "Sometimes we have lots of cash and other times not a cent. And yet our profit and loss statement for the first year looks good."

"I know," said Cathy. "And now that we've put out cash for the bears, what about the rent due next week?"

"Wait," said Madeline. "We've got the charge card slips to bring to the bank, so we should be O.K."

"I forgot about that. What a relief! But we can't keep on like this. There must be a way of knowing what cash we will need and when and from where it will come."

The above is a classic situation of a small business showing a profit yet having cash availability problems. Cathy asked if there was a way of knowing ahead of time what cash would be needed and when and from where it would come. Yes, there is a way. It is called cash management.

WHAT IS CASH MANAGEMENT?

When we talk about cash, we are referring to the money a business has in its till, in petty cash, or in the bank. There are basically two reasons why a business must have sufficient cash on hand:

• to be able to pay regular bills and other expenses when they come due
• to account for uncertainties and faulty estimates of planned expenses

Insufficient cash can result in serious problems. The extreme result is, of course, the business's insolvency. A less serious result is having to delay paying your bills. The inability to pay quickly will first mean the loss of any supplier's discounts on invoices that are paid promptly (e.g. 2% discount if paid within 10 days of invoice date). Secondly, consistent delays in repayment will eventually affect the credit rating you have with your suppliers.

Holding too much cash, however, is also not recommended.

Too much money means that your cash resources are not being used to their best potential. Money that sits idle ultimately costs you money. How? It costs you money if it does not earn interest; if by sitting idle for a long period of time it is affected by inflation; and, if it is not used to pay liabilities that are incurring interest charges.

Of course, it is better to have too much money than too little. It is even better to have the right amount. Cash management determines, as accurately as possible, what the cash balance should be at all times.

Cash management can be divided into two activities: regular controls and the cash flow forecast.

Regular controls of your cash are:

a) **At the till** — till and tape balances should be balanced. Cheques, which you may want to personally approve before they are honoured, should be deposited with your bank as soon as possible.

b) **At the petty cash box** — you will want to ensure that the amount which you have set as a petty cash reserve is always there in either cash or vouchers.

c) **At the bank** — you will want to reconcile your records and your bank's records of deposits and withdrawals, and provide for cheques which you have issued but which have not yet reached your bank.

The cash flow forecast, which is also referred to as a cash flow budget, can be described as:

• Showing, on a month to month basis, what cash you estimate to receive, what cash you will have to pay out and where you may have cash surpluses or shortages.

Let us next look at how a cash flow forecast is prepared.

PREPARING A CASH FLOW FORECAST

Basically the cash flow forecast or cash flow budget simply illustrates the flow of cash through a business for a future period of time, usually six to twelve months. In other words, it shows when cash will be received and the amount, and when cash will be paid and the amount, for this prescribed period of time. A cash flow forecast is usually divided by months.

Here is an example of a cash flow forecast. Not all of the lines are applicable to every small business, but the majority of them can be completed.

Cash Flow Forecast
for the period _____

	Jan.	Feb.	March
Add Cash Receipts:			
Cash from Sales			
Cash from Receivables			
Loan Proceeds			
Cash from Other Sources	_____	_____	_____
Total Receipts	_____	_____	_____
Less Disbursements:			
Improvements			
Fixtures			
Equipment			
Inventory			
Management Salaries & Taxes			
Employee Wages & Taxes			
Rent			
Mortgage Payments			
Heat, Light & Power			
Office Expenses			
Maintenance & Repairs			
Advertising			
Insurance			
Legal & Audit Fees			
Miscellaneous Expenses			
Loan Repayment			
Income Taxes	_____	_____	_____
Total Disbursements	_____	_____	_____
Cash Surplus (Shortage)	_____	_____	_____
Cash on Hand:			
Beginning of Month			
End of Month			

Let us review the sample cash flow forecast line by line.

Cash from Sales   Use this line for sales that will generate immediate cash during the month. In other words, the customer pays cash, by cheque, or by charge card for merchandise or services purchased from you.

Cash from Receivables   This line is for sales that have been taken on credit. The actual sales may be one or two months previously, but this is the month when you expect to receive the cash. For example, if your terms are 30 days and a sale took place January 15th, you would forecast payment to be received in mid February. Note that your cash from receivables will vary markedly at certain periods of the year due to seasonal buying habits.

Loan Proceeds   If you will receive the proceeds of a loan, such as a line of credit, the amount will be shown on this line for the appropriate month. It is this line that would show the financing arrangement that you have made to cover any cash shortages.

Cash from Other Sources   This line accounts for any cash received that is separate to the proceeds of a loan or the monies directly generated by your business operation. This line could be used to show the sale of fixed assets and equipment or to show the proceeds of an additional investment from a partner or major shareholder.

Total Receipts   Here you put the total of all the cash anticipated to be received by the business during the month.

Improvements, Fixtures, Equipment   These are capital expenditures and should be shown in the month that payment for them will be made. Normally, these are disbursements that are not a constant monthly expense.

Inventory   This entry shows when the inventory purchased is to be paid for. It is not when the inventory is received, unless you are on a COD basis. Your inventory must be determined in relationship to your sales forecast.

Depending on your type of business, inventory purchases also can vary from month to month.

Management Salaries & Taxes Employee Wages & Taxes
These two entries include the income taxes and fringe benefits paid by the business on the employee's behalf. In principle, the owner's or owners' salaries are included as an operating expense. When determining the monthly amounts, keep in mind seasonal slack and peak periods or situations where an increased wage force is in direct relation to increased sales.

Rent Mortgage Payment
This is usually an either/or situation. Each month should include any interest or escalation charges as well.

Heat, Light & Power Office Expenses Maintenance & Repairs Advertising Insurance Legal & Audit Fees Miscellaneous Expenses
These form the bulk of your operating expenses. Again, your type of operation, location, etc. will dictate whether or not, and when, any of these expenses will vary. Insurance, as well as legal and audit fees, may be paid on a monthly basis throughout the year or may be a once only payment.

Loan Repayment
Here, you show the repayment of your loan — principal and interest. If the loan was for the purchase of a fixed asset, then the monthly payment will probably be a specified amount. If you have a line of credit, the repayments will more than likely vary each month.

Income Taxes
This is your estimate of what taxes will be payable and when. This line may be completed monthly or on a periodic basis if you pay taxes by installments.

Total Disbursements
This is the total of all cash anticipated to be paid out by the business during the month.

Cash Surplus	Here, you show the difference between total receipts
(Shortage)	and total disbursements. If your receipts exceed your
	disbursements then you will show a surplus for the
	month. If the disbursements exceed the receipts
	then there is a shortage for the month.

Cash on Hand — This is the amount of money available at the end of
Beginning of the previous month.
Month

Cash on Hand — This is the amount of money at the end of the current
End of Month month after adding the surplus to the beginning of
the month line, or after subtracting the shortage from
the beginning of the month line. This amount becomes the cash on hand — beginning of the month
line for the following month.

NOTE: The **Cash on Hand — End of Month** line is the most important
part of your forecast. If your estimate shows a negative balance,
you will have to borrow this amount of money to meet your
planned expenditures.

A cash flow forecast is to be referred to, and worked with, often. It
is not just done once and then left in a file. To derive maximum usage,
you should review and adjust each month to reflect any changes in
either cash receipts or cash disbursements. These changes may be either
in amount or in time.

Remember, a cash flow forecast to really help must be accurate
and must be used. It is the most important tool that you have in cash
management. As well as helping you in assessing cash needs, it may also
be requested by a term lender when considering your proposal for a loan.

CONCLUSION

A business can operate profitably and yet have difficulties because it is starved for cash at certain times of the year. Good cash management in the form of regular controls and a cash flow forecast will help alleviate this situation.

Instituting cash handling practices and checks or audits such as bank reconciliations allow you to keep on top of your daily cash activity. These are your regular controls. Your cash flow forecast predicts where and when cash shortages or excesses will occur. This allows you to plan ahead.

Cash is one of your business's most vital assets. It must be managed well.

10. GIVING CREDIT TO YOUR CUSTOMERS

"The granting of credit has both a positive and negative side. Good credit management helps ensure the positive side."
— *CASE Counsellor*

INTRODUCTION

Credit has been defined as the ability to obtain goods or services in return for a promise to pay in the future. It is a sale on trust. But how can you be sure who, among your customers, is trustworthy, and who is not? There are ways to find out. How much credit should you extend to those you trust? Again, there are ways to determine such limits.

As a business owner or manager, you should be familiar with sound credit management principles and how to apply them to your own business practice. This is the purpose of our chapter.

THE ADVANTAGES OF OFFERING CREDIT

The principal advantage of offering credit is that it increases sales.

Granting credit allows goods or services to be purchased by customers who would otherwise be unable to do so, or who would purchase the same goods or services from others willing to offer credit. Sales are increased not only by widening the customer base to include such customers among your clientele, but also by that group as an entity. These people who purchase on credit tend to buy more goods and services, and more frequently.

Customers to whom credit is given often develop a loyalty to the firm that has invested its trust in them. They will generally return to that firm first before making purchases elsewhere. The advantages of giving credit, therefore, are:

- increased sales
- increased customer base
- a competitive edge over businesses not granting credit
- customer loyalty

THE DISADVANTAGES OF OFFERING CREDIT

The main disadvantage of offering credit is the cost to the seller.

When selling on credit, a business is giving away its product for only a fraction of its cost. Payment in full will not be received immediately, but the costs of producing the product must nevertheless be paid by the seller. The effect is the same as making a loan to the customer. Therefore, a greater amount of capital must be available to the business than would be required if operating solely on a cash basis. The cost of this capital is an added expense to the seller.

In addition to the cost of the greater amount of capital, there are the costs of determining which customers are worthy of credit, costs of maintaining records of amounts owing, and costs of billing and collecting. And no matter how careful you are in granting credit, there will likely be customers who will fail to pay; the resulting bad debt is yet another expense.

Other disadvantages to granting credit are: the higher rate of returns or exchanges of goods since customers who buy on credit are more likely to return the goods; overbuying of goods that the customer does not need and cannot afford; overselling by the seller. All these factors contribute to higher costs to the seller.

YOUR CREDIT POLICY

You have weighed the advantages of offering credit to your customers against the disadvantages. You have chosen to offer credit. Where do you start?

You start with a policy which you can set for yourself and your business. Your credit extension policy should be neither too liberal, nor too restrictive. Too liberal a policy invites excessive receivables and uncollectible accounts while an overly restrictive policy can lose you potential sales.

A successful credit and collection policy requires that all problems be detected and dealt with as early as possible. Accounts that become too long overdue often become uncollectible.

1. Average collection period

An important indicator of the effectiveness of your credit and collection policy is your average collection period. The average collection period is a ratio that expresses the total amount of receivables outstanding in terms of an equivalent number of average daily credit sales.

The average collection period is calculated by dividing your accounts receivable by the average daily credit sales:

$$\frac{\text{Accounts Receivable}}{\text{Average Daily Credit Sales}} = \text{Average Collection Period}$$

Let us take an example. If a business has average monthly credit sales of $12,000 and outstanding accounts receivable of $18,000, the collection period would be calculated as follows:

$$\frac{\text{Average Monthly Credit Sales}}{30} = \text{Average Daily Credit Sales}$$

$$\frac{\$12,000}{30} = \$400 \text{ (Average Daily Credit Sales)}$$

Returning to the original equation:

$$\text{Average Collection Period} = \frac{\$18,000}{\$400} = 45 \text{ days}$$

This is the indicator. It shows that, on the average, customers are taking 45 days to pay their accounts. Other formulas used to calculate the average collection period consider only net sales. These are determined by subtracting an estimated allowance for bad debts from total annual credit sales.

Once your average collection period has been determined, it can then be compared with any of the following bases to spot a potential trouble source.

Payment terms   If your terms of sale specify payment within 30 days and your average collection period is more than this, it indicates that creditors are not complying with your terms, and a problem exists.

Past history   Comparison with results in past periods indicates whether collections are improving or declining.

Industry averages   Comparison with the experience of other companies in your industry will determine whether or not your credit and collection policies are as efficient as theirs. Industry averages can be obtained through trade associations and government bulletins.

2. Keeping receivables in line

The same equation, Average Collection Period = Accounts Receivable ÷ Average Daily Credit Sales, can be used to determine if your receivables are excessive when compared with the industry's average collection period.

For example, assume that your terms of sale specify payment within 30 days, and that your industry average collection period is also 30 days. A suitable target for your receivables would then be 30 days' average credit sales. If your average daily credit sales are $400, you could then calculate a target for receivables as follows:

$$\text{Average Daily Credit Sales} \times \text{Collection Period} = \text{Accts. Receivable}$$
$$\$400 \times 30 = \$12,000$$

If your actual receivables were $18,000, you would then know that you had an average of $6,000 ($18,000 − $12,000) in receivables that must be dealt with on a priority basis.

How do you do this? You would immediately reduce the collection period, speed conversion of receivables to cash, minimize your capital tied up in accounts receivable and, in the process of doing so, reduce the risk of uncollectible accounts.

3. Set your terms

Your credit extension policy should specify the terms you are prepared to offer your customers, and what limits will apply. Those terms and limits should be clearly stated on the invoices you send to your customers. Is payment due within 10 days or 30 days? Are the days measured from the receipt of goods, receipt of the invoice, or the end of the month?

4. Cash discounts

If your credit-granting competitors are offering a cash discount to their customers, your credit extension policy should also include such an offering.

The cash discount, usually one or two percent, for payment within ten days, is usually indicated as follows: 2/10

The first number is the discount percentage: 2%. The second number denotes the number of days within which the payment must be made in order to take advantage of the discount. Thus the term, 2/10, means that the customer can take a two percent discount for payment within 10 days.

But this is 10 days from when? If the customer lets the discount period slip by, when is the net amount due? The answers are specified in the dating terms which can be noted as follows: 2/10 — n30

The n signifies net. The 30 denotes the number of days within which period payment is due. If no other date is indicated, the 30-day period begins with the invoice date. Thus, if the terms above were indicated on an invoice dated June 16, the customer would be entitled to a two percent cash discount for payment on, or before, June 26. If the customer does not pay within this period, the net amount is due within 30 days, or by July 16.

5. Monthly statements

You should send monthly statements to your customers to advise them of their account balances. The statement should clearly indicate the amount owed and show any transactions that have taken place in the account during the 30-day period.

If you choose not to use the invoice date as the beginning of the dating period, either one of two abbreviations, EOM (End of Month) and ROG (Receipt of Goods), should be clearly indicated on your invoice. EOM means that the discount and net periods begin at the end of the month, regardless of the invoice date. ROG signifies that the period begins when the customer receives the goods, regardless of the invoice date.

Returning to the preceding example, if the following was noted on your invoice: 2/10 — n30 EOM, the customer would then be entitled to a two percent discount for payment by July 10. If your customer chooses to disregard your discount terms, the net amount would be due July 30.

Your competition may force you to offer the same payment terms as they have; so before choosing a particular set of terms, find out what your competition is offering.

6. Delinquency charge

In your credit extension and collection policy, you may wish to establish a delinquency charge for late payment. The purpose of this is to discourage your customers from allowing their accounts to become long overdue.

The delinquency charge takes the form of a service charge, expressed as a monthly percentage in line with current interest rates, on all balances more than 30 days past due. The charge should be noted as such in the monthly statement you send to your customer. Refer to the charge as a late payment rather than a delinquency charge.

YOUR COLLECTION POLICY

A cardinal rule of good receivables-management is to minimize the time span between the sale and the collection. Any delays that widen the span cause receivables to grow to even higher levels, thereby increasing the risk of the account becoming uncollectible.

The best time to begin collecting long overdue receivables is always NOW. If the overdue account is difficult for the customer to pay off now, it will only be more difficult in the future if it is allowed to languish in your books.

You should, therefore, establish a firm collection policy, and stick to it even if it means upsetting a so-called good customer. No customer whose bills are rarely paid according to your credit policy is good. Don't worry about the customer not coming back should you press for payment of the outstanding balance. The customer whose account is cleared is more likely to return to do business with you again than the one who is badly in arrears. Don't be concerned about unreliable customers giving you a bad reputation because of your collection policy. Customers who are bad debtors will not want to reveal this fact.

It is unrealistic to think that you will not have bad debtors when you offer credit. You may be a good judge of character, but last year's good customer is as capable as you are of falling on bad times.

Take the case of Fred Krantz whose small snowshoe fabricating operation could barely keep pace with the demand for the handmade product. He made every effort to complete Marcel Gauthier's order simply because Marcel had been one of his first customers, and had doubled his orders every year for the preceding four years. Marcel ran a sporting goods store and ski repair shop at one of the busiest ski hills in the Laurentians.

Then this winter, what little snow fell was washed away by rains. Marcel's accounts, not only with Fred but with other suppliers, became delinquent. Had Fred been wrong to have extended Marcel so much credit? After all, Marcel had proved his reliability on previous orders. The answer is yes. Fred knows, as well as Marcel, what a poor winter can do to business. Fred knew Marcel, but did he know how prudently Marcel was running his business? If he didn't, he could have found out.

Our next section examines how the small business operator can obtain credit information.

CREDIT INVESTIGATIONS

Three sources of credit information are available to the business owner without a credit department which could normally carry out a credit investigation. They are: Credit Bureaus, Better Business Bureaus, and Dun & Bradstreet.

Credit Bureaus In Canada since 1922, now have over 150 branches and a staff in excess of two thousand to provide businesses with consumer credit records of individuals.

Credit Bureaus basically confirm information that credit grantors (banks, mortgage companies, department stores, oil companies, finance companies, and automobile dealers) have obtained from individuals requesting consumer credit. Under Canada's consumer credit laws any individual applying for credit must do so in writing. When a consumer does this, he not only supplies information such as details of identification, present and past addresses, present and past employment, salaries and references to the grantor but, at the same time, agrees to his application being checked. The Credit Bureaus build up this information with reports of other credit requests by the consumer, turn-downs of credit as well as payment histories obtained from existing accounts where credit was granted.

Other information on the Credit Bureaus' files — not supplied from the credit grantors — is derived from the public record: judgments, non-responsibility notices, registered chattel mortgages, conditional sales, and bankruptcies.

Files are only opened on individuals when a request for information is received from a credit grantor or when something appears on the public record. The Credit Bureaus stress they do not grant credit; they merely advise and provide assistance to those in business to grant credit.

To use the Credit Bureaus' services, a business must apply to the nearest Credit Bureau and, depending on whether the business's market is local or national, take out a membership fee ($25 or $100). With the annual membership comes a special code number which allows the business to telephone the Credit Bureau and obtain verbal reports on individuals. A nominal fee is charged for each report. Written reports can also be obtained.

When information is already on file, the verbal report is instantaneous; otherwise, if a new file has to be opened the verbal report is generally given within 24 hours. Credit Bureaus in Canada are associated with their U.S. counterparts (3500 Bureaus) and in Europe.

Credit Bureaus point out that they provide counselling service on credit to businesses; that most bureaus issue a monthly bulletin which provides up-to-date information on the credit industry applicable to the local area; and that, while primarily their credit reporting pertained exclusively to individuals, retail and commercial concerns are now being filed (a different fee structure is applicable for retail and commercial reports).

Better Business Bureaus There are 14 in Canada, serving 68% of the market population, and incorporated as non-profit organizations — they do not provide credit information on companies or individuals. Instead they compile business reliability reports that include a grading system of 1-A to D.

Information in these reliability reports is mainly of two sorts:
• basic information which comes from the company itself
• information about how the company has handled complaints forwarded to it by the Better Business Bureau

These reports come into being through both outside initiative: information enquiries, complaints, public record, as well as internal initiative: a local Better Business Bureau contacting a company suggesting a voluntary listing in the bureau's files.

The Better Business Bureau, when complaints are received about a company, will vet the complaint, and then pass the complaint on to the company in question. The disposition of the complaint, whether adjusted, disputed, or rejected as unjustified, is tabulated on the company's reliability report and is the prime factor in setting the bureau's rating system on a company.

A rating of 1-A means that no complaints have been received on the company; an A rating shows that a company examines and adjusts a large majority of valid complaints; B rating means the company has only 50-60 percent rate of adjusting valid complaints; both C and D indicate that the company does not meet the bureau's standards.

Though the Better Business Bureau invites companies to become members of its organization, anyone can request a verbal reliability report. Reports are available both on member and non-member companies. The bureaus in Canada are in contact with nearly 150 Better Business Bureaus in the United States.

Dun & Bradstreet Canada Limited Eleven offices across the country which provide credit and financial reporting in the form of Business Information Reports and the D & B Reference Book.

Dun & Bradstreet business reporters gather and interpret essential credit background information on the management and activities of manufacturers, wholesalers, retailers, and business service industries. The information obtained includes the history, operation, payment record, finances and banking of a business; all of which is summarized into report form and used as the basis for assigning a rating on the credit-worthiness of the business.

The majority of this information is obtained voluntarily from businesses themselves. Most companies recognize that it is better to supply Dun & Bradstreet with full and accurate information resulting in a correct rating than run the risk of their file not being complete or current. Additional information is obtained from banks, suppliers to the company, and the public record. Once a file is opened on a company it is kept in a process of update.

The Dun & Bradstreet rating is composed of two parts: (1) estimated financial strength, and; (2) composite credit appraisal. The estimated financial strength of a company is shown as being between a minimum and a maximum bracket (example: rating DD $35,000 to $49,999). The composite credit appraisal, divided into classifications of high, good, fair and limited, represents an assessment of a company's credit-worthiness that has considered such factors as management, survival and growth ability, and payment records.

The D & B Reference Book, which is revised every two months, is a listing of over 380,000 Canadian businesses. Each listing includes the business name, year started and D & B rating. The Reference Book has been designed as a convenient source of preliminary information to check small orders, set up credit lines based on ratings, and to note business changes with customers and prospects.

A business wishing to use the services of Dun & Bradstreet must take out a yearly subscription. This entitles them to verbal and written Business Information Reports on companies (75% of requests answered immediately from files; reports sent on the balance of enquiries within one to six days) and the D & B Reference Book.

THE CREDIT APPLICATION

There's a fourth source of credit information you should refer to even before you consult the previously mentioned outside sources. That is the credit application itself.

A credit application should tell you three things you must know before you grant the applicant credit:

- the applicant's ability to pay based on income and obligations
- the applicant's reliability in meeting credit obligations
- the potential profitability of the account. You stand to lose your cost of the product or service if your customer cannot meet payments. If your cost is relatively high compared to the selling price, then you have to obtain as many facts about the applicant as you can.

For individual applicants, you should know the following:

- employment history
- current occupation
- current income
- length of time in current occupation
- security of the job
- monthly expenses such as rent, utilities, food budget, etc.
- bank balance
- personal possessions such as house, car, investments, etc.
- credit standing
- amount of credit requested

Information on the first five will likely give you a good insight into the three C's of the applicant's credit-worthiness: character, capacity, and capital.

If the applicant is employed, his or her immediate supervisor, or a personnel supervisor, can reveal details about the applicant's character and capacity (ability to assume obligations, financial and otherwise). The applicant's banker cannot divulge details about the applicant's bank balance, but can discuss the credit-worthiness of the applicant as it relates to his or her performance in paying off past or present bank loans.

You should feel free to ask why the applicant needs credit. If it is due solely to a cash shortage, and your investigation reveals that the applicant has held a steady job and has met all financial obligations in the past, then that person is likely to be an excellent credit risk. If the applicant is short of cash and is overextended elsewhere, this indicates a poor risk.

There are no infallible guidelines to spot good or poor risks. There are poor people who always pay their bills, and there are rich people who do not. A combination of facts and figuring will point the way; if hunches in the past have proven to be right, keep responding to them.

A TEST OF PROMPTNESS

In agreeing to grant credit to an applicant, you should explain clearly your policy terms, and you should set a credit limit **based on the customer's ability to pay**. A cash down payment on certain types of merchandise is a practical deterrent to unnecessary or excessive purchases.

A test of promptness in meeting your terms begins with you, the creditor. A delay in sending your invoices will likely be met with a delay in receiving payments. You will set the example of promptness with your customers. If you neglect to apply a delinquency charge, your customers will likely neglect to get their payments back in line. Firmness will bring results.

CREDIT CARD SERVICES

If you are managing the kind of business that has a large number of relatively small accounts, credit arrangements for customers are available through use of credit cards. Two major credit cards are offered through Canadian banks. There is, of course, a charge to the seller for the use of the credit card system. This is expressed as a percentage of the sale. The percentage will vary depending on the overall volume of sales that you have.

Credit card services eliminate the need for credit approval, invoice preparation, record maintenance, and collections. They also minimize your commitment of capital and virtually eliminate the risk of uncollectible accounts. From a marketing standpoint, the availability of instant credit often encourages a customer to buy immediately rather than postpone a decision to buy, or dismiss the impulse completely.

CONCLUSION

Buying on credit is very much a part of the Canadian economy and has become a major factor in doing business. Therefore, all businesses at some time will have to consider the granting of credit.

Yes, there are risks to giving credit, but the rewards will outweigh them if you establish a sound extension and collection policy that is tailored to the needs of your business. Once the policy is established, **you** must adhere to it or your customers will not.

11. PAYING YOUR EMPLOYEES

"How you pay your employees is a reflection on their performance and the performance of your business."

— *CASE Counsellor*

INTRODUCTION

The most sensitive issue in business is employee recognition. You recognize the contributions of your employees in two basic ways: praise (positive feedback) and pay. Often the former can be a substitute for the latter, but not for long. An employee who is underpaid and over-praised will put up with the situation where genuine self-sacrifice is called for, such as when sales nosedive due to an unexpected crisis imposed by external economic conditions. But when a business is prospering, as most should, employees will also expect to prosper. Failing to recognize them by paying them wages and salaries that reflect their contributions to that prosperity will lead to a downfall — in morale and productivity.

What you pay your employees is more than a reflection of their performance, however. It is a reflection of business conditions. And you should be as aware of these business conditions as you are of the employees' performance.

PREPARE A POLICY

You often hear employees complain of being overworked, but seldom of being overpaid. Like their employers, they mentally relate the work they put into the job to the remuneration received. Most employees know when they are being fairly paid for their labours; but when they feel they are being poorly paid, they often retaliate by performing lackadaisically, arriving late for work, taking long coffee and lunch breaks, and frequently phoning in sick.

Formulating a wage and salary policy and making employees aware of it can prevent a decline in morale and productivity.

Jack Baker paid the price for not having such a policy. He owned a shoe store in a small Ontario town, and had the good fortune of having Fred Kealy as an assistant. Where Jack was inclined to worry, Fred was carefree and always jovial with the customers. His joviality took a nosedive when Jack hired Karen Harwood, fresh out of high school. Fred felt that his special position in the business was threatened, but within days he too fell under the spell of Karen's bubbly enthusiasm for people pleasing as she called it.

Business was brisk that summer and fall. At Christmas, Jack privately gave Fred and Karen an envelope with a Christmas bonus as a way of thanking them for their efforts in increasing sales to over 12 percent above the previous year's record.

A few days later, Karen told Fred what she had bought with her bonus, and it occurred to Fred that she had been given the same amount as he had, and once more he felt a sense of betrayal. After all, she had only begun in June, five months short of a full year, and yet had been given the same amount that he had received for a full year's effort.

Fred finally built up enough courage to complain to Jack.

"I don't think it is fair," said Fred, "Karen got the same amount of bonus as I did. She's had no previous experience; she's half my age, and she's been here for only seven months."

Jack was perplexed as to what to reply.

"I don't pay a bonus based on a person's years, experience, or age. Karen was paid not only to sell but also to do the window displays. Those two jobs are equivalent to a year's work. Don't forget your salary is higher than hers."

Fred didn't say anything more, but he remained unhappy for three or four weeks. Jack resented the suspicion of favouritism and wondered if he had given enough thought to the whole question of remuneration for employees. Maybe he should establish policies that would avoid problems such as the question of a bonus.

Policies — written and adhered to — not only avoid employee-management problems, they also establish the rules of the game. If everyone knows the rules, the game can be played as it should be.

THE POLICY

Wage and salary policies should contain neither generalizations like "Top dollar for top work", nor specifics such as actual amounts like "Up to $20,000 plus commission for all sales positions".

A policy can be summed up in one or two clearly worded sentences.

For a small firm, a policy might resemble that of O'Connor Clothes. Owner and manager, Stan O'Connor, drew up this policy when he hired the first of the four employees he brought into the business.

It reads as follows:

O'Connor Clothes

"Wages and Salaries: It is the policy of O'Connor Clothes to pay its employees the average of rates for similar work in this community, to comply with all applicable wage legislation such as minimum wage and vacation pay legislation and to review wages and individual performance at least once a year."

At first glance, the wording seems trite, but note a few key phrases: average of rates, similar work, comply with ... minimum wage ... legislation. O'Connor Clothes doesn't pay higher than average wages; it pays average wages — as a matter of policy. It doesn't pay as well as any employer in town; it pays the average for clothing stores in town — as a matter of policy. It pays above the minimum wage and is committed to do this if the minimum wage increases — as a matter of policy. It considers raises, based on how well the employee does his or her job, at least once a year — as a matter of policy.

Stan O'Connor's policy, stated in writing, clears the air — for himself and his employees. There can be no clouds of suspicion. It is there in black and white.

FROM POLICY TO PRACTICE

Having a wage and salary policy is like having a car in your garage representing your transportation policy. Putting it to use is the real measure of its worth.

Like a car which is the embodiment of up-to-date engineering and design principles, a wage and salary policy is the embodiment of current principles of remuneration, among them:

The going rate — what the competition is paying for similar work. If you offer less, expect to get less qualified employees, or less productivity from them.

Legislated rates — what governments decree that you must pay (minimum wage, vacation pay, termination pay).

Job description — the duties the job entails. More duties generally mean more pay.

Job evaluation — the worth of each of the duties the job entails. Specialized skills command a higher rate than general skills.

Performance appraisal — how the employee performs relative to the job description and evaluation.

Wage and salary revision — when forces beyond your control — government regulation, union settlements, or competitors — raise wage rates, you must revise yours accordingly.

Knowing these principles, let us see how they should be applied to actual pay practices.

The going rate   As a business owner, it will not take you very long to find out what your competitors are paying for similar work. Your employees will let you know. Where matters of pay are concerned, they keep themselves informed. But always verify an employee claim such as, "They're paying thirty percent more at Oswald's across town." Check with Oswald's to confirm. As well, call two or three other businesses comparable to yours. If you're shy about making a direct inquiry, keep your eye on the employment ads in your newspaper. Your competitors will often include the salary range for the job they are advertising. Clip the ad out for future reference. Other sources of information on salaries are your Board of Trade which publishes annual wage surveys, and your provincial departments of industry, trade and commerce.

Legislated rates You are dissatisfied with the employee you hired three weeks ago. What termination and holiday pay do you owe him? Your provincial government has very specific policies governing such situations. You can find out by getting onto the mailing list of the Canada Department of Labour which publishes "Labour Standards in Canada", a booklet detailing minimum wage rates for all provinces, including pending changes in such rates. Also consult your provincial labour relations authorities.

Job description In small businesses, these can be written on a single page. In large businesses, they can stretch to ten pages. Ideally, job descriptions should include, in addition to the duties involved: a general description of the function to be performed; a definition of the authority which the job is given in order to achieve its objectives: reporting relationships to you directly, or to your second in command; standards of performance, e.g. incumbent must close an average of five sales a week.

Job evaluation Is a typist who types twenty business letters a day worth more or less than a bookkeeper who comes in only two days a week to perform an equally necessary function? In small businesses with only three or four types of jobs, the owner can rank them reasonably accurately. In larger businesses, a point system is used.

Performance appraisal Performance appraisals are both informal, and formal. Informal appraisals involve day-to-day contact with the employees during which you, the manager, can observe their strengths and weaknesses as they perform their duties. Improvements can be suggested on the spot but this should always be done in private. At least once a year, generally on the anniversary of the employee's employment date, you should make a formal appraisal. On that occasion, the employee's performance is measured against his or her job description to determine how effectively the duties are undertaken. The appraisal should record the strengths of the employee as well as the weaknesses, so that next year's appraisal can focus on the efforts to overcome these weaknesses.

Wage and salary revision   Occasionally external factors beyond your control will oblige you to revise an employee's salary to reflect changing conditions in the workforce. The government might revise its minimum wage rate, or the largest employer in town might suddenly advertise for welders at rates twenty percent higher than what you are paying. In the latter instance, you are not obliged to revise your welder's salary to match your competitor's, but failure to make some comparable adjustment in direct wages or fringe benefits could lead to problems with your employees.

How would Stan O'Connor apply these principles in his pay policy towards his employees?

Let us take the case of Doris Vines, Stan's most experienced saleslady. Doris joined O'Connor Clothes five years ago as a salesperson, having previously worked at Eaton's in the town's major shopping centre. She is now paid $180 per week, or $9,360 per year. It is time for Stan O'Connor to review her performance over the past year. How might he do this?

Let us listen in on their private exchange.

"Doris," says Stan genially, "you've been a great help during the past year. Always ready to pitch in. I hear the sales people at Eaton's got a raise."

"Going to match it?" she asks.

"Better than that. I'm going to go one better. But it will require that you take on an additional supervisory role. Interested?"

"Well, being the senior salesperson here, I've always tended to Mother Hen them, sometimes to the point of ruffling their feathers. So I'll be glad to have my role formalized, so to speak."

"Well, for your new responsibilities, I'm offering you $40 more a week. How's that sound?"

"It sounds great," she replies.

It's all there: the going rate, wage and salary revision, job description, job evaluation, and performance appraisal.

Doris was given a raise based on a change in the prevailing rates in the job market, her own good performance during the past year, and increased responsibility.

The principles of a sound wage and salary policy were put into practice. And a sound employer-employee relationship continues.

REASONS FOR RAISES

Raises can't be given in a spirit of generosity. Not even Santa Claus gives gifts to those who haven't deserved them. He only rewards for good behaviour. But an employer must take other factors than just good behaviour into consideration before he passes out his annual gift of a pay raise.

In brief, they are:

- the ability of the business to pay increased wages
- the basic job requirements
- internal pay relationships
- performance
- cost of living trends
- supply and demand for employees
- rates of pay in other organizations
- wage indices and trends

Let us take a closer look at these considerations.

The ability of the business to pay increased wages Wages are paid out of the business's revenues. If raises are to be given, there must be at least a proportionate increase in the business's sales volume or its prices, or a proportionate decrease in operating costs. In a company where machines rather than people do most of the work, such as a photocopy firm, the wages of the firm might account for 10 percent of the cost of the product. A 10-percent wage increase would add one percent to the production cost. In a service business, such as a travel agency, wages might account for 80 percent of the firm's cost. A 10-percent wage increase would raise costs by eight percent.

The basic job requirements   What does the job require of the employee, and what are the requirements worth to the success of the business? A specialized skill commands a higher wage than does a generalized skill. The employee who can repair television sets, as well as sell them, should be paid more than the employee who only sells them. Why? Because the former brings two skills to the business: technical and sales.

Internal pay relationships   What is the relationship of one employee's pay to another in the same business? Should the salesperson who brings $40,000 in sales to the firm be given a greater raise than the delivery person who brings no sales to the company, but renders a necessary customer service with cheerfulness and enthusiasm?

The dilemma is not impossible to solve. All the employer needs to do is to appraise each employee's performance. If each has performed to capacity, they each get a similar raise, say 10 percent. The amounts will vary obviously, but the increase will be fair to both.

Performance   Always keep in mind that you appraise an employee's performance in terms of his or her job description, not in terms of the performances of others in the company. The delivery employee might not have contributed directly to sales, so there shouldn't be any judgment relative to these other employees. But the delivery person might have boosted customer relations with an obliging manner, and that's an indirect contribution to sales. Satisfied customers will keep patronizing the firm.

When an employee performs well in terms of the objectives laid down in his or her job description, but is now at the top of the pay range for the particular job, it is time to consider a promotion to another job or to more senior responsibilities within that job classification. This is what Stan O'Connor did with Doris Vines.

Where performance cannot be rewarded with a promotion, you may wish to consider giving the employee a bonus. A bonus should be awarded on the basis of the business's profitability and the employee's contribution to it.

Cost of living trends In recent years, cost of living allowance (COLA) clauses have been written into union-negotiated contracts, and non-unionized employees have come to expect that the same factor be included in any pay raise, irrespective of performance. But if the cost of living increases 10 percent in a 12-month period, the employee who has performed indifferently should not expect to get an automatic increase of 10 percent. High wages for low productivity is a major cause of inflation and the ever-increasing cost of living.

Supply and demand for employees One of the rules of the marketplace is that prices go up when supplies are limited, and fall when supplies are plentiful. But in the job market, this law doesn't necessarily apply. An employer may offer a high salary for a job and still get few applicants. On the other hand, minimum wage regulations will prevent him from lowering the wage for a job that fifty eager applicants desire. When the salary that the employer offers does not draw interested applicants, it should be either increased or, if that is not possible, the job description should be revised to include attractive fringe benefits in lieu of salary.

Rates of pay in other organizations When comparing rates of pay with those for similar jobs in other businesses, make sure that the businesses are similar in most ways. You cannot compare a unionized plant with a non-unionized plant, nor a 10-employee manufacturing firm with a 10-employee retail firm. The wages of the key employees in each business often affect the wages of the support staff, so that a typist in one kind of business may receive a wage much higher than that of a typist in another business which offers a very different kind of product or service. The employer should be aware of pay rates in similar businesses, but shouldn't slavishly match them unless employment conditions are absolutely identical.

Wage indices and trends These are publicized in a variety of government and institutional reports. It can be helpful for the small business person to know the forecasted wage trends for particular segments of the workforce. If a steep rise is forecasted within the months ahead, now may be the opportunity to consider an increase in wages to ensure loyalty.

COMPUTING A PAY RAISE

How do you decide on the exact amount of an individual pay increase?

If you have done the kind of investigation previously suggested (i.e. compared wage rates for similar jobs in similar organizations, checked the sources forecasting the anticipated cost of living, and the supply and demand for the kind of skilled workers you require for your firm's successful operation) you are ready to conduct private performance appraisals with each employee on your staff.

Let us return to O'Connor Clothes. There we learned that Stan has obtained figures on actual salaries paid to salespersons by five employers in his community. They ranged from $3.60 per hour to $190 per week. In all cases, the work week was 40 hours. Stan converted these figures to annual salaries because all his budget figures and other financial data were expressed in annual figures. The wage range that emerged ran from $7,488 to $9,880 with a mid point of $8,684.

Stan interpreted this as meaning that starting rates clustered toward the bottom of this range, that those who did an average job would likely progress from the starting to the middle point, and perhaps higher, and that a salesperson who showed above-average performance should be paid a wage near the top of the range. He also knew that such a range would gradually change, likely upward, and that the whole range would need to be reviewed at least every year.

In essence, he had this picture:

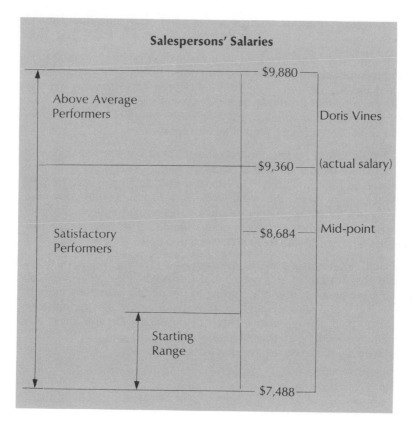

Salespersons' Salaries

Above Average Performers

$9,880

Doris Vines

$9,360 — (actual salary)

Satisfactory Performers

$8,684 — Mid-point

Starting Range

$7,488

What factors did Stan have to consider in revising the wage and salary of Doris Vines? The first one was her added responsibilities. If she was to take on a supervisory role over the other salespersons, she would no longer be doing the same job as they were. She would be doing more, and therefore, should be paid more. Stan got Doris to agree to have three more duties added to her job description:

1. supervises the quantity and quality of the work of all the salespersons
2. trains new salespersons
3. reports to me on the work of all salespersons

Stan also changed the job title or classification to: sales supervisor.

As far as Doris' performance was concerned, Stan regarded it as above average. Stan reasoned that based on her new responsibilities, performance, and comparisons with other employers, her salary should be above the top of the range paid to salespersons, that is $9,880, by at least eight to ten percent. She had not received a pay increase for 12 months, and during that time the Consumer Price Index had increased by nine percent. Unemployment in the area had practically disappeared because of the opening of a new radio and television assembly plant. Stan realized that he needed Doris Vines on his staff, and even though she was already the highest paid of his salespersons, she should receive the promotion and pay increase.

Stan had to consider other factors. Ten percent above $9,880 would be $10,868. This would be slightly more than 16 percent over Doris' present rate of $9,360. Stan wondered what would happen if all his costs were to rise 16 percent per year. He certainly couldn't increase his prices that much. Doris needed a nine percent increase just to catch up with inflation. He realized that income taxes would erode part of her increase, too. She had no formal experience in supervising, so would have to begin at the lower end of the salary range for sales supervisors. Granting Doris a $40 per week raise which is a 22.2 percent increase over present salary seems excessive, but not in light of the increased responsibilities she will assume. It is the kind of raise that not only will motivate her, but will likely lead to increased sales by her staff as a result of her imparting to them her renewed enthusiasm and dedication.

CONCLUSION

All businesses, whether large or small, should have a written, clearly worded wages and salary policy accessible to all employees. Initially, the owner/manager will determine the policy. As the number of employees grows, the policy may be revised through collective bargaining.

The small business owner must take into consideration eight factors when determining the extent of pay increases. They are:

1. the ability of the business to pay increased wages
2. the basic job requirements
3. internal pay relationships
4. performance
5. cost of living trends
6. supply and demand for employees
7. rates of pay in other organizations
8. wages indices and trends

The first four are internal factors; the last four, external. Keeping these factors in mind when applying the principles of a wage and salary policy to individual cases will pay off in terms of good employee relations.

12. PERSONNEL RECORDS

"A good system of personnel records will show, on any day, accurately and quickly the number of employees you have, who they are, what job each one has, how much each one earns, and where each employee is located."

— *CASE Counsellor*

INTRODUCTION

Just as a bill of sale is created the moment you sell some merchandise or a service, a personnel record is created the moment an employee is hired. And like bills of sale which identify the item or service, the date of sale, and the amount of the sale plus sales tax if applicable, personnel records identify the new employee and record the date of the person's entry into the firm, the amount to be paid in wages or salary, and personal income tax exemptions.

This chapter examines personnel records by dividing them into three distinct sections: general files, personal files, and the payroll record. As well, we look at the reasons for having personnel files and the requirements for their retention.

WHY KEEP PERSONNEL RECORDS?

Why should you, a business owner, keep personnel records? There are two major reasons:

• sound business practice recommends that you do
• governments **insist** that you do

Because you must keep personnel records, it makes sense to organize a system that serves your purposes as well as those of your employees and the government.

Amber Ogilvy, owner of Forever Amber Fashions, prided herself on her memory, and she had reason to do so. She could remember the wholesale prices she had paid for a particular manufacturer's blouses six years ago when she opened her boutique. She could remember the amount of the loss she took when she overestimated the demand by her clientele for peasant-look ensembles.

Despite her memory for prices, profits, and losses, Amber couldn't remember everything, even though she thought she could. This was proven when Judy Garrett, her top salesperson, turned petulant toward her in late June, and remained that way for days. Amber finally took her aside to ask what the problem was.

"Well," said Judy sulkily, "I was hoping you would announce my raise. It's been three weeks, now."

"Three weeks? What has been three weeks?"

"Since my fifth anniversary of the day I joined up with you."

"Why didn't you remind me? I've been so involved with ordering for our fall line, I completely forgot."

"Well, you always hate to be reminded of things. But I did think you'd remember my anniversary. You did last year."

"Well, I can't be expected to remember everything all the time!"

No, she can't. That's why she should have made a record of it. Not only has she disappointed her best salesperson who was hoping for an acknowledgement of her fifth anniversary, but she has also missed conducting a performance appraisal to coincide with the anniversary of the starting date of her employee. This was a habit that Amber had always managed to keep until now. As well, Judy has not been informed of the amount of her raise, which is generally revealed at the conclusion of a performance appraisal.

Another reason for keeping such records is that both provincial and federal governments require that an employer maintains clear and complete personnel records. A typical directive from a government department dealing with employees and employers reads in part:

"An employer _____ shall make and keep, or cause to be made and kept, for a period of at least _____ months after work is performed by an employee, a record of the name, address, wage rate, vacations with pay or payment in lieu of vacations, hours worked and actual earnings of the employee and such other information as the regulations may require."

A final reason for keeping personnel records is that you might be asked to give a reference concerning the work history of an employee who worked for you three or four years previously. You might be asked by your Board of Trade to provide data on employee turnover in small businesses like your own, or for information on salary and wage scales in your organization.

WHAT ARE PERSONNEL RECORDS?

For ease of reference, we have divided personnel records into: **general files**, **personal files**, and **payroll records**.

1. General Files

General files comprise files on such topics as recruiting, training, manpower planning, salary administration, forecasts, budgets, and benefit plans just to mention a few. They should be accessible to any employee seeking information on such topics. Simple file folders can be used to contain material either drawn up by the employer (e.g. policies on specific subjects such as wages and salaries) or received from various government agencies. A brochure describing imminent shortages of manpower for selected skills and trades should be retained in the manpower planning folder for future reference.

The size and scope of the general files depend on the attitude of the employer towards storing information. Some employers like to keep bulging files on every business subject just in case, which might be a hoped-for invitation to speak to members of the local Chamber of Commerce, or to deliver an address at an assembly of high school students on Business Day.

Other employers prefer to keep information stored in their heads, then discard the material after a quick glance. This could become an unsound business practice.

Time is more expensive to a business person than a filing cabinet. Retaining information in the general files might prove to be more time-saving than making hurried telephone calls or writing letters to government departments or business organizations asking them for information they have already sent to you.

2. Personal Files

These files contain confidential information on employees. Unlike general files, personal files must be kept under lock and key so as to ensure the employees' rights to privacy. The law also states that an employee has the right to see his or her own personal file. Personal files must also be kept for government purposes.

A personal file can contain:

Correspondence A letter to the employer requesting employment; reference letters; a letter from a doctor advising the employer to grant the employee sick leave; a letter from the employee to the employer registering a grievance.

Documents Photocopy of the employee's birth certificate; transcripts of high school, junior college, or university grades; photocopy of the employee's driver's license (when the employee uses his or her own vehicle or the firm's vehicle on the job).

Photo Generally, a duplicate of the photo which appears on the company identification card.

Job Description For the owner of a business with fewer than five employees, a job description mainly comprising a list of the employee's duties can be written on a single sheet of paper. A job description is necessary for the employer and employee. This ensures that there is no misunderstanding about what is expected of the employee. A job description is used as a reference for determining the quality of the employee's performance in carrying out the duties listed.

Performance Appraisals Performance appraisals, generally conducted on the anniversary of the employee's first working day, contain evaluations — from poor to good to excellent — of performance relative to the duties listed in the employee's job description. Performance appraisals should not only evaluate past performance, but should set new goals for the year ahead. They should be retained to determine whether or not the employee has performed effectively in meeting those goals.

Application for Employment Form Small business owners often prefer to avoid the formality of filling out an application form. They simply hire on the spot, judging the applicant on appearance and personality. But failing to check the oral claims of previous work experience could lead to on-the-job conflicts. For example, the owner discovers that the applicant can, in fact, type, but too slowly for the requirements of the position. Checking with the employer of the firm where the candidate claims to have worked will quickly reveal the competence of the applicant. If an owner decides to draw up a form, to be photocopied, and then handed to applicants when they present themselves, it must be kept in mind that government fair employment regulations serve to eliminate job discrimination against non-Caucasians, females where they are able to perform the duties of a traditionally male-dominated position, the mature job-seeker, the handicapped, and members of minority religions within the community.

The owner is entitled to information concerning the applicant's name, mailing address, telephone number, social insurance number, education, and work history.

An employment record (card or sheet)   The purpose of this kind of record is to have readily available each employee's name, address, social insurance number, and job and wage record. When the employee's job, location or wage rate changes, the record should be updated. Though this kind of record can be kept on cards in a file box, a regular 8 1/2″ × 11″ sheet is more convenient because it contains more space for recording changes, and it fits neatly into a regular file folder. Should you design such a sheet for your personal files, remember that there are three main changes of status which can occur during a person's employment. An employee may:

• change duties
• relocate within the organization
• end employment (resign, retire or be terminated)

Ideally, on any given day, your records should show how many employees you have, who they are, what job each has, and where each is located. Obviously, it is easy to keep such information accurate and up-to-date if you have only five employees at one location. It becomes more complex if you have fifteen permanent and six temporary employees at two locations, as well as a high rate of staff turnover. But such complexity is the very reason for maintaining personal files. It eliminates mental recall, and ensures accuracy when reviewing the work history of employees.

148

Here is an example of the kind of employment record sheet that a small business owner could devise for use in the personal files.

TYPICAL SMALL BUSINESS
Employment Record

Family Name: . . . .   First Name . . . .

Address: _____   _____   _____

            _____   _____   _____

            _____   _____   _____

Telephone: _____   _____   _____

Social Insurance Number: _____

	Education	**Work History**		

Date	**Job Classification**	**Location**	**Wage/Salary**	**Remarks**

3. Payroll Records

Some of the information to be found in the employee's personal file must also be entered in another kind of personnel record: payroll records.

There is a large variety of payroll forms and stationery available to businesses, but the main objectives of all payroll records are:

- to calculate the gross pay (regular and overtime) for each employee before the end of each pay period, the deductions to be made by the employer as required by law (e.g. employee income tax instalments) or by the authorization of the employee (e.g. employee contributions to a savings plan or a charity fund), and the net pay

- to pay each employee his or her net pay at the end of each pay period (e.g. every two weeks or twice monthly)

- to maintain a continuous permanent record of all payroll transactions, including individual changes in pay rates

Whichever format your payroll records take, the following information about the employee must be entered:

- complete identification of employee — name, address, social insurance number, date of entry into your organization, personal income tax exemptions

- pay period (e.g. every second Thursday)

- gross salary

- net salary

- deductions — the most common payroll deductions are:
  - provincial and federal income tax instalments
  - government pension plan contributions (federal and Quebec)
  - contributions to employer's pension plan
  - unemployment insurance premiums
  - contributions to group life insurance plans
  - contributions to medical insurance plans
  - union dues

— payroll savings plans
— contributions to charity appeals

Almost eight percent of businesses in Canada have less than a dozen employees. The owner, therefore, can devise a fairly simple, inexpensive payroll records system. We illustrate two forms that could be used by the small business person. One is a **payroll sheet** which is completed for each employee; the other is a **payroll summary sheet** completed at every pay period.

If the business were to increase the number of employees, or if the owner becomes too occupied with other matters relating to the business's growth, payroll services offered by banks and other similar firms can be used at generally reasonable rates.

PAYROLL SHEET (FOR EACH EMPLOYEE)

NAME: _____ ADDRESS: _____ PHONE: _____

SOC. INS. NO.: _____ EXEMPTIONS: FEDERAL: _____ PROVINCIAL: _____

POSITION: _____ SALARY: _____ DATE STARTED: _____

19—	Hours Worked							Rate	Gross Earnings	FED Tax	PROV Tax (Que only)	UIC	Pension (CPP or QPP)	Medi-care	Other	TOTAL Deductions	NET Earnings	Cheque No.
	M	T	W	T	F	S	S											
JAN																		
Total																		
FEB																		

PAYROLL SUMMARY SHEET (FOR EACH PAYDAY)

EMPLOYEE NAMES	Gross Earnings	FED Tax	PROV Tax (Que only)	UIC	Pension (CPP or QPP)	Medicare	Other	TOTAL Deductions	NET Earnings
Total									

KEEPING PERSONNEL RECORDS UP-TO-DATE

Keeping records up-to-date takes time; but on the positive side, it saves time. An example of saving time is when you need up-to-date information immediately and you do not have to take time searching for it or checking its accuracy.

Ensuring that your records are **clear, complete, convenient**, and **confidential** will go a long way in helping you keep up-to-date. Your records should be:

Clear   Is the address that is scribbled on this scrap of paper your employee's old address or new address? It will be clear if you have devised an employment record sheet that contains space for more than one change of address.

Complete   If you were forced to discipline an employee for an infraction, jot down the complete details of the act, and the action you took as a corrective measure. You might need the details if the employee files a complaint with a union or the provincial ombudsman or human rights commission. Your records might indicate your fairness in your handling of the incident.

Convenient   Records are designed to serve, not sink you. If you devise your own forms, make sure that they contain as much information on a single sheet as possible, to save you from having to add more sheets. Example: as mentioned above, making space on an employment record sheet for changes of address will save you from having to devise a change of address form.

Confidential   Most information about your employees is personal, so keep your personal files under lock and key.

Governments, as we have noted, require that the employer maintain personnel records. If a government department (Ministry of Labour) or board (Workmen's Compensation Board) were to ask for copies of the personnel records of one of your former employees, would the records be complete? If not, would you be able to recall specific details of the employee's work history in order to make them complete? On such occasions, you might find yourself wasting precious hours, even days, getting information on the employee that would have taken only minutes to record when the changes in that person's wages and work routine took place.

If you, the employer, do not have the time to keep your personnel records up-to-date, delegate the duty to someone who has the time.

Keep in mind that updating records is almost always done in conjunction with another activity that involves having an employee's personal file before you. At the time you appraise an on-the-job performance, and inform the employee of the changes in duties and salary or wages, simply record the changes on the appropriate sheets in the file. It's that simple and quick. You are prone to error if you do not immediately record changes in wages or a job classification.

RETAINING PERSONNEL RECORDS: FOR HOW LONG?

What should you do with personnel records that you no longer need? You will eventually destroy them; but only **after** you have confirmed that they are obsolete.

When an employee leaves your business, don't immediately destroy that person's file. Simply switch it to an inactive file. There are many reasons that it should not be destroyed immediately. These include requests for references, year-end income tax returns, enquiries from the former employee and, most importantly, laws from the governments stating the periods of retention. These periods of retention specified by the governments can range from one to five years.

An inactive file should only be destroyed when you are permitted by law to do so. Once you have established the date that the file can be destroyed, write that date on the file where it is clearly visible. That will help you weed out a file when you come across it after the date it was to be destroyed.

Records of job applicants are another story. If you interview fifteen applicants for one job, you will likely have fourteen forms that aren't of long-term interest. Your interview notes and references or other materials submitted by the applicants might be attached to the form. Some of the material might have to be mailed back to the applicants. If you wish to keep some of the applications for consideration for other jobs in the future, insert them in a file labelled promising applicants or whatever you feel describes them best. Keep the others in a file denoting rejected applications for no longer than a year. Applicants who re-apply over a year later should be asked to fill out new forms.

CONCLUSION

As a good manager, you will wish to be in control of all your assets. Assets include your personnel. So keeping control of, and monitoring, this asset called personnel will mean a certain amount of record keeping. This record keeping, or personnel records, is both a necessity and a legal requirement in operating your business. Keep your records clear, complete, convenient, and confidential so that they will serve their purpose — and yours.